BELLYDANCE

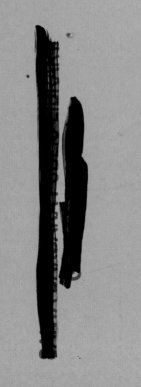

KETI SHARIF

BELLYDANCE

A GUIDE TO MIDDLE EASTERN DANCE, ITS MUSIC, ITS CULTURE AND COSTUME

ALLEN&UNWIN

First published in 2004

Allen & Unwin
83 Alexander Street
Crows Nest NSW 2065
Australia
Phone: (61 2) 8425 0100
Fax: (61 2) 9906 2218
Email: info@allenandunwin.com
Web: www.allenandunwin.com

National Library of Australia
Cataloguing-in-Publication entry:

Sharif, Keti.
    Bellydance : a guide to Middle Eastern dance, its music, culture and costume.

    ISBN 1 74114 376 4.

    1. Belly dance. 2. Belly dance music. 3. Costume - Middle East. 4. Middle East - social life and customs. I. Title.

793.3

Photography credits: Gulda Quinn, Panizza De Rossario, Dick Stein (rstein@bigpond.net.au),
Dale Neill (www.fotograf.com.au), Craig Kinder and Emma van Dordrecht.

Text design by Tabitha King

Set in 10/15 pt Futura
Printed by Everbest Printing Co. Ltd., China

10 9 8 7 6 5 4 3 2 1

CONTENTS

ACKNOWLEDGMENTS

There are many people to thank for inspiring this guide—musicians, dancers, students, choreographers and countless others who have shared their knowledge, observations and passion.

Special thanks to all the photographers who have donated their stunning images of the dance. To Michèle Drouart for inspiring me to collate my ideas into a book and to all my bellydance colleagues around the world for their continual support and enthusiasm.

I also wish to express my gratitude to the many fine teachers of Middle Eastern dance who have shared their knowledge with me over the years, especially Hossam Ramzy and Mahmoud Reda.

Keti

Keti Sharif

$\mathscr{I}$NTRODUCTION

Bellydancing is an ancient art—existing for thousands of years in the Middle East—yet relatively new in the West. Anyone growing up in the West before the last few decades would have been unlikely to see much in the way of bellydance. However, with the increasingly multicultural make-up of western societies, we have had the good fortune to be exposed to the arts of many different countries. My own story is a case in point. I grew up in Australia and did not become involved with bellydance until I was seventeen years old, when I was mesmerised by a Macedonian gypsy dancer named Esma—the first bellydancer I had ever seen. Her confidence and femininity overstepped even the bounds of the Slavic culture of my own family. She had the spirit of the East. Her influence and my growing passion for the dance led me ultimately to study with choreographers in Cairo, where I later danced as a professional performer at the Ramses Hilton. The immersion in Egyptian culture taught me that dance is not for the stage only. It is a means of communication between people. I began to understand that it could also contribute to communication between cultures.

On my return to Australia, I studied the origins of the dances, and this eventually led me to research ancient dance sites in Turkey for a cultural course I was developing for my students. I have since been back to Turkey to live in the south-eastern part of the country where folkloric dance was predominant. My more intimate experience of the life of the people there, and in other places like the villages of Egypt, Jordan, Greece and Morocco, expanded my view of women's dance in the Middle East. With my growing involvement in the preparation of this course it became evident that its premises and emphasis would have to be post-orientalist. The current worldwide resurgence of interest in traditional Eastern dance, instead of 'othering' and exoticising, goes hand in hand with a desire to understand the spirit of the people who created it.

Bellydance shifts constantly in form and style: earthy and tribal at one point, folkloric at another, or turning to cabaret. As a teacher of bellydance in a Western country, I see an increasing number of women coming to learn this beautiful art every year. They are eager to discover the different styles of dance throughout the Middle East and are often surprised that the cultural stylisations differ so greatly from what they had originally perceived. Still more surprising, the colour, the grace, the humour and sensuality weave a tapestry of expression that empowers women in the West.

In 1998 I had the good fortune to host two of the world's leading instructors of Egyptian dance: musical composer and dance teacher, Hossam Ramzy with his wife Serena, and master choreographer, Mahmoud Reda, on separate tours of Australia. Hossam and Serena Ramzy's workshops focused on musical interpretation and the traditional 'baladi' sentiment. A pioneer of 'world music', Hossam has revived many Egyptian classics, inspiring a global interest in Egyptian music. Mahmoud Reda taught the many provincial dances intrinsic to various parts of his country; his research of traditional dance, music and costume has been a lifelong project that spanned five decades and has taken Egyptian dance to the main stages around the world. When we are fortunate enough to meet them, observe them and listen to them, we can learn about bellydancing from the people of the Middle East.

I have written *Bellydance* as a tribute to Middle Eastern dance and a celebration of its splendour, as well as of the dancer's art.

Part one

DANCE OF THE EAST

1

'AHLAN WA SAHLAN'
WELCOME FROM THE MIDDLE EAST

The world of bellydance in the Middle East is mysterious and alluring. For centuries it has heralded events controlled by the life force and life cycle such as the growth of new crops, the birth of a baby, the wedding of two lovers—events associated with fertility. Could this be why it is a realm of feminine power and sensuality? In the modest societies where it originated, and often hidden behind veils, bellydance is a surprising bounty of feminine expression. The dance arts of the East, enjoyed by men and women alike, are synonymous with festivity and celebration, but the feminine style of dance known as 'oriental dance' in the Middle East, or 'bellydance' in the West, has survived the longest. The jubilant nature of bellydance is fuelled by spontaneity, passion and a sense of fun. No occasion for celebration is missed in the Middle East—celebration with heady rhythms and joyous dance!

Bellydancing is an expressive art that manifests itself early in the lives of Middle Eastern women. The dance has raised women from their cushions and rugs, enticing them to sway a little, laugh a little—giving them a podium to perform the steps they have known since childhood. Little girls charm the family when they mimic their mother and sisters with a sweet and awkward sway of the hips. In adolescence, the long, warm mornings they spend sipping mint tea are spiced with intermittent displays of movements that combine to form a playfully confident art shared among generations of women. Weddings, parties and the gathering of family and friends justify the indulgence of dance, the opportunity to show off a hip move or a shimmy.

3

In the Middle East, many women are naturally wonderful dancers, yet whilst dance is accepted as a creative pastime in the home, families discourage their daughters from pursuing it as a profession. Public dance performance is censured for its earthy sensuality and associated with the 'sins of the flesh' that inevitably bring about the demise of society. The public dancer may be the daughter of a poor but musical family, entertaining at local weddings—though never invited as a guest. Because of her profession, she remains a citizen of low social status, unless she becomes famous. Ironically, the top oriental dance performers in the Middle East are national icons. These glamorous women enter the league of the famous at cosmopolitan five-star hotels in cities like Cairo, Beirut or Istanbul. Their careers usually expand into cinema and television, where they acquire further wealth and fame. Decorated with jewels and expensive fabrics, the celebrated dancer symbolises through her art the beauty within every woman. From a Western point of view, the social stigma attached to the 'dancer/performer' in the East is a perplexing phenomenon, all the more so because it can suddenly turn into adulation.

Centuries ago, throughout the Middle East, the tribal dancer who celebrated the simple world of harvest and religion through ritualistic song and dance became the traveller's muse. Exotic, caramel-skinned dancers of the Ouled Naïl people intrigued painters and poets who sought the romanticism of the East . . . and brought it to the West. And in our own times the Egyptian cinema industry modernised the 'bint al balad', the native country girl who learnt her dance from her mother and grandmother in a small clay dwelling in the desert before her generation moved to the city to find work. Through migration, modernisation, westernisation and other cultural influences, the bellydance of the East evolved stylistically. All of these contributed to our witnessing of countless varieties and concepts of Middle Eastern dance.

Music, dance and rhythm have always been part of Middle Eastern culture. In a spread of countries over three continents, the styles of dance are as diverse as the many cultures occupying the land. From the Bedouin dancers in colourful kaftans to the baladi

3

dancers of urban Cairo, folkloric traditions have survived the generations. Throughout the Middle East—from Turkey through Egypt to Morocco—free-form bellydance retains its exuberant, feminine quality and continues to be noted for its interpretive artistry. While this dance varies from region to region, its breadth transcends class and culture. In Cairo there is a saying: 'Every girl is born a dancer.' This popularity of dance at all levels of society suggests it is an intrinsic part of life, whether in the home, on the Nile riverbank or in the nightclubs of the five-star hotels.

The women of the Middle East, to whom this dance belongs, use it to celebrate their bodies and to communicate a powerful message bequeathed to them by their ancestors. They remind us that beyond the confines of society, this is a dance for the spirit.

'ORIGINALLY, PEOPLE DANCED THEIR DANCES

AS AN EXPRESSION OF THEIR DAILY LIVES, FEELINGS,

VALUES AND SOMETHING WE CALL "TRADITION".'

CLAIRE NAFFAH, LEBANON

2
HISTORY

The postures and movements of bellydancing have a long and interesting history. Anthropologists have suggested that dance was a form of ritual celebration of fertility from the time of the Upper Palaeolithic age, from around 30 000 BC. Since the finding of the 'Venus of Wilendorf' sculpture dated at approximately 25 000 BC, some of the world's oldest artefacts have depicted the female figure—often in postures similar to those used in today's bellydance. As art has always reflected society's primary concerns, we can assume that ancient female iconography portraying dance suggested a religious, if not spiritual, connection between femininity, dance and fertility. The wall paintings of dancers in the old Neolithic shrines of Catal Huyuk in Turkey (6000 BC) are further evidence of this.

From around 4000 BC, early civilisations that originated in the Middle East, like the Sumerian, Babylonian and Assyrian cultures, worshipped female deities. Mythology born of this era focused on the 'birth dance'—a celebration dance that formed a direct relationship between the seasonal, cyclic fertility of women and the fertility of the earth. The biblical 'dance of the seven veils', which many associate with the tempestuous nature of bellydance, is believed to be an aberration of the myth of the 'dance of shalom' (literally the 'welcome dance'), associated with the deity Ishtar. The mythology of Ishtar revolves around the goddess as representative of the seasonal birth and death of vegetation. Ishtar's descent into the underworld is reflected in the barren winter, and her ascent in the rebirth that commences in the spring—hence the name 'welcome dance'. The mythology tells of her journey into the underworld, where she shed seven attributes, later metaphorically called veils, in order to pass through the gates of that world and save her husband, Tammuz. Many myths and legends can be traced back to the eras between 4000 BC and 500 BC, when feminine-based religions worshipping a 'mother figure' abounded.

There were many pre-Christian and pre-Islamic religions that involved dance as part of religious worship. One can still visit the ruins of old temples and amphitheatres in Turkey and Greece, where priestesses once danced during the reign of the matriarchal religions, devoted to figureheads like Artemis, the virgin goddess of the hunt, and Aphrodite, the goddess of love. During the same era, dance also evolved within the Egyptian Pharaonic dynasties. Predynastic Egypt, around 4000 BC, was an agricultural society, but from around 2700 BC it rapidly developed into a cosmopolitan one where philosophy and the arts, including dance, flourished. Images like 'The Banquet' from the tomb of Netumun, dated at 1400 BC, illustrate the development of choreography and music in Egyptian culture. From this early era in Egyptian history, dance has featured prominently as a stylised entertainment art.

Since the days of the spice route, the Middle East has been a central site of cultural exchange. Persians, Ottoman Turks, Phoenicians, Indians and Spaniards have warred and traded throughout the area known as the Levant, and their legacy has been a fusion of cultures and of art. In the area of dance, the ancient Indian temple dancers, for example, are believed to have inspired the ornamented dances of the Middle East. Nomadic gypsies, travelling the vast expanse of desert, can be traced back through their genealogy to India. Their form of dance brought much of the lively spirit still seen today at weddings, births, festivals and other celebrations. Many Middle Easterners like to claim that gypsies—'Cengi' to the Turks or 'Ghawazee' to the Egyptians—are responsible for the more lewd and suggestive styles of bellydance.

Since the advent of the patriarchal religions of Christianity and Islam, women's dance has been viewed with a mixture of fascination and contempt. The dancer/entertainer tended to be well versed in storytelling and a consummate musician who became a courtesan or concubine. Yet, regarded as a violator of fundamental religious laws, the female dancer was often outcast, sometimes even replaced by male khawals (impersonators of female dance). From the harems of the Ottoman Empire, where oriental dance flourished, to the traditions of the prostitute–dancers of the Ouled Naïl in the Sahara desert, women's dance became the cutting edge of sensual expression. Even non-dancers in this otherwise strict society, somehow kept traditional bellydance alive in the confines of their homes for generations.

In some cultures, certain genres of dance were still viewed as an art form. In Egypt, female intellectuals that became 'Almeh', or 'learned' dancers, were highly sought after as entertainers, especially for weddings and festive celebrations. The mature Almeh trained the highest quality troupes, and were therefore respected in society. The Almeh and other 'high society' dancers became the Western artist's muse as the West's fascination with the East developed into the burgeoning orientalism of the eighteenth and nineteenth centuries. European artists and travellers brought back tales of opulent harems and dancing girls, and the 'odalisque' became the single most influential icon in European art during that time.

It is generally believed that when Turkish dancers were brought to the San Francisco Fair of 1889 the French term *danse du ventre* (meaning 'dance of the belly') was adopted by the Americans and translated into 'bellydance'. Since then, bellydance has become a popular theme to represent the 'exotic East', both in movies and on stage, from famous stage performers of the time, like Little Egypt or Oscar Wilde's character, Salome, to Mata Hari.

Many Western notions of the orientalised bellydancer—for instance, that she is always dressed in a sparkling two-piece costume—were in fact Hollywood inventions. More fascinating still—and something of an irony—is that the East favoured the glamorous new look and adapted it to suit their flourishing cinema industry!

Over the previous century, the constantly evolving art of bellydance, from traditional to cabaret, has undergone a greater number of shifts and changes than ever before. The dance has journeyed to every continent on the planet and has been kept alive through both original cultural migrants and keen enthusiasts. Indeed, the concept of bellydancing has often been misunderstood, westernised and de-authenticated; yet we could look at this expansive dance as a starting point for many other varieties of human expression and actually as an improvised art, a theatrical inspiration, a healing and therapeutic practice and a cultural study.

Bellydancing has always fascinated both the East and the West. It is also an art that continues to grow, and makes the best advances with an understanding of the basic sources of the dance—the music, the rhythm, the people, the stories and the moves.

3

MUSIC AND INSTRUMENTS

Middle Eastern music is an expressive language of quarter tones and percussive rhythms, varying from slow and sensual to upbeat and playful. The patterns are simple, yet dynamic, and there is always room for improvisation—hence the 'felt' or emotive quality characteristic of Middle Eastern music. The traditional instruments have ancient origins, dating back to predynastic Egypt. Today, they accompany the accordion, saxophone, violin, cello, clarinet and other orchestral instruments. The orchestras in the Middle East are very large. Sometimes an orchestra of 30 musicians plays for a solo dancer. Recently, electronic instruments like the keyboard, synthesiser and guitar have been used to replicate the sounds of traditional instruments.

The following are brief descriptions of some of the most common Middle Eastern instruments, though there are many others. For the dancer each instrument tends to resonate with a certain part of the body or instigates a particular move in bellydancing, and these moves, too, have been outlined.

Wind instruments

Nay   A reed flute used in Turkish, Arabic and Persian music. It produces haunting, wavering, breathy notes and exudes an ethereal quality that suggests lightness. The dancer usually responds with her arms and upper body or with the veil. In Turkey, it is played for the spiritual whirling of the 'mervlana' or dervishes.

Kawala

A flute played in Arabic and Turkish music. The 'kavala' (Turkish pronunciation) originated as a shepherd's pastoral calling instrument, and because of this quality often participates in call-and-response instrumentals. Although it usually sounds playful and light, being higher-pitched than the nay, it can also produce a soulful, wailing sound that affects, for the dancer, the upper body and arms.

Arghul

A double-reed pipe, also called an 'Egyptian oboe'. It looks like an oboe but the arghul, like the kawala, can produce a soulful, wailing sound similar to that of a clarinet, but more nasal. The dancer can perform sinewy, snake-like movements to its smooth melodies.

Mizmar

An Arabic horn that produces a sound like the drone of Scottish bagpipes, but loud and trumpeting. It is often played for the Saiidi cane dance of Upper Egypt. The sound has a vitality and energy that synchronises with the lifting of the arms, the twirling of the cane or full, body-turning movements. The Turkish equivalent is called the siz.

Stringed instruments

Oud

A pear-shaped wooden lute similar to a guitar, played with a plectrum. The name means, literally, 'flexible stick'. The oud is intrinsic to Middle Eastern dance music, creating both melody with its notes and rhythm with the strumming style. The sounds of the lute family bring life and energy to the music, affecting the middle of the body. The dancer usually responds with soft shimmies or figure-eight movements with the hips and torso. The oud instrumentals of Farid El Attrache are excellent for bellydancing.

Bazouki

The Greek version of the oud. It is a smaller, longer-necked lute popular in the chiftetelli style of music (of Turkish origin), and is often played tremolando throughout an entire piece.

Saz

A very long-necked lute from Turkey that is played tremolando for the Turkish chiftetelli. The dancer often responds with a shimmy movement in the shoulders or hips, or curling inward figure-eights that Turkish dancers call 'lakoum'—meaning 'Turkish delight'.

Rababa

A very early version of a violin. It has a coconut shell for the body, with horsehair strings attached to a long neck, and is played while the musician is seated. The sliding horsehair bow over the strings produces notes similar to the sound of 'a swarm of mosquitoes or bees'! Traditionally, the rababa was one of the leading instruments played in Egyptian, Persian and Turkish folk music. Nowadays, it is often replaced by the violin in the classical orchestra.

Qanoon

An Arabic and Turkish dulcimer. Also known by its Greek name 'zither', this is a harp-like instrument made of wood, usually walnut. The body acts as a resonator for the 72–78 horsehair or metal strings. Qanoon literally means 'the law', as it controls the Arabic takht (acoustic wooden ensemble) for both the dancer and the musicians. It is an instrument with a sensitive quality, best played in solo improvisation. The gentle tremolando signals to the dancer to vibrate hips and belly, with the intensity of vibration depending on that of the strums.

Similar in design to the qanoon, but struck with wooden mallets, like a xylophone. The santoor produces a surprisingly playful sound that induces accents and shimmies.

Percussion
Darbuka/tabla

A Middle Eastern drum. The darbuka, from the Arabic word 'daraba' ('to strike'), is known as a 'tabla' to the Egyptians. It began as a drum with a hollow clay base covered in fish or animal skin. Nowadays, the darbuka can sport a wooden base covered with attractive mother-of pearl or made from tougher alloy. A modern plastic skin and adjustable rim are convenient, as they are more durable and easier to tighten, tune or replace. The darbuka, played open-handed, produces a variety of tones, from a deep, base tone—called a 'dom'—created by striking close to the centre, to a light treble sound—called a 'tak'—produced by striking the rim. When these main doms and taks are arranged in special combinations, the resulting series of Middle Eastern rhythms can be the basis for an emotive dance balad or a climatic 'drum solo'. From surprising accents to rolling shimmies, the darbuka gives the percussion section, and the dancer's hips, personality!

Dumbek

The metal goblet-shaped drum popular in Turkish and Persian music. It cannot be played in the same way as the darbuka because of its hard metal rim. The drummer clicks and rolls their fingers over the skin covering the dumbek to produce the 'rolling' taks, and still plays the doms by striking the centre. The dancer responds with hip movements similar to the moves used for a tabla—shimmies and hip accents.

QANOON

DOF

Doholla
The Arabic-made version of the tabla—a bigger, thicker-skinned drum that sets the pace of the rhythm, giving it body and strength. Footwork and weighty moves often respond to the deep, hollow rhythm of the doholla.

Mazhar
A drum from the tambourine family with rows of metal cymbals around the edge, and played up close to the shoulders. It creates a steady rhythmic tinkering that makes the dancer enliven her routine with shimmies—mostly performed in the upper body, but also in the hips.

Dof
A drum from the tambourine family, but without cymbals. It is also played up close to the shoulders. It creates a lively rhythm with a rap-a-tap that gets the dancer's shoulders and hips moving. Sometimes the Egyptian baladi dancer will use the dof while she dances.

Maktoum
A large, round-based drum played between the knees, also known as a 'katem', meaning 'background'. The maktoum plays only part of the rhythm—the bass, giving it strength and dynamism. It is an underlying rhythm that the dancer can follow with her hips or with the stepping of her feet.

Tabul
An enormous drum from the tambourine family, played low, often strapped to the drummer's body, so the free hands can pummel the skin

with padded sticks. It produces a heavy bass sound and keeps a steady rhythm that is popular in Egyptian Saiidi and Lebanese dabke folk-dance styles. The drummer can walk when playing this big drum, and often leads a wedding procession.

Reque

A light tambourine with layers of cymbals, which produces a delicate sound. The dancer often responds with shoulder shimmies.

Zills

The Turkish name for small metal finger cymbals, also known as 'sagat' in Arabic. The dancer wears them over the thumb and middle finger of each hand and plays them by striking together the rims of each pair. In this way the dancer embellishes the music with light tinkering rhythmic patterns. In Egypt, a percussionist in the orchestra plays large cymbals called 'toura'.

4

MUSICAL INTERPRETATION

Bellydancing is traditionally performed to Middle Eastern music and rhythms with a series of sensuous, supple and flowing moves. In this interpretive art, the dancer becomes a physical manifestation of the music. The dancer uses her body—as musicians use their flutes, drums and oud—to express the emotive and rhythmic elements of a composition. For instance, a dancer responds to fast and joyous music with brisk movements that express gaiety and celebration, yet when the music becomes slow and sensual, her body reflects the mood with a slow style of improvised dance called 'taqsim'. Usually, the melody creates the emotive atmosphere, while the rhythm governs the speed and momentum of the piece.

Bellydance music employs many modes of composition, where instrumental dialogue prompts the dancer to respond accordingly. Here are some modes of Middle Eastern music the dancer should listen for:

- Taqsim—Musical improvisations where the dancer uses only part of her body in response to the melody of the solo instrument. She holds the move for as long as the note's duration.
- Call-and-response—Where the dancer performs a 'question and answer' series of movements, relating to the 'conversation' between the instruments.
- Repetitive rhythmic—Where the dancer repeats appropriate steps, hip moves or sequences of movements that weave well together. This often follows the 'rule of four'(p 24).

- Accents—These prompt short, sharp movements exactly on the beat. Accents are particularly important in the darbuka/tabla solo sections.
- Full orchestration—Where all the instruments come together to create a musical picture or story. The dancer often responds with larger, 'spatial' moves like turns, gliding steps or sweeping gestures.

Although bellydancing is largely intuitive, the dancer can interpret the musical moods of a composition by better understanding the effects of the instruments. Snake-like figure-eights suit the serpentine sound of the arghul, while a rapid beating of the darbuka prompts a shimmy of the hips. A slow, sensual tempo invites undulations and the tremolando sound of the qanoon encourages a gentle tremble of the hips and belly. The dancer holds the move for the duration of the note. Long notes are best interpreted with flowing moves, while sharp, staccato notes suit quick moves and accents. Generally, solo instruments are easily read for their singular emotive qualities. The dancer often demonstrates them in a stationary position, using the corresponding part of her body to interpret the 'feel' of the sound. Yet when many instruments are played together, their fullness often suggests broader sweeps of movement, like travelling steps and turns.

Egyptian dancer Mervat at the Cairo Marriot

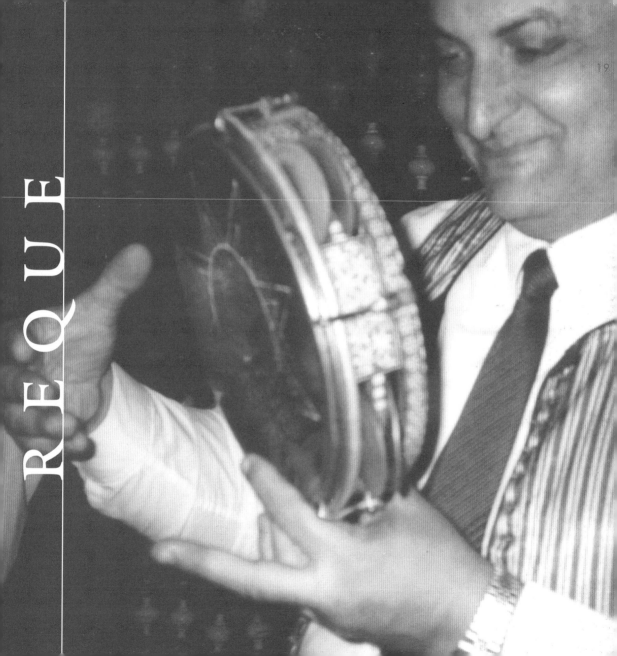

REQUE

The Element of Air

The wind instruments—the flute family, including the nay, kawala, arghul and mizmar—are all instruments of the air. They rely on the breath to create sound. They are physically played high in the body and their sound suggests lightness. The element of air communicates freedom, lightness and spirituality. The gestures that best correspond to the playing of air-element instruments are upper body movements—arms, shoulders, head and upper torso. The floating weightlessness of the nay suggests delicate arm and hand moves, lifting the arms high to replicate the direction of the sound.

Ancient Persian music and Sufi traditions incorporate the nay in their spiritual music. The sharper sounding kawala also suggests arm, hand and upper body moves. Wind instruments that produce a deeper sound, like the arghul, are well matched by snake arms, shoulder rolls and the swaying of the upper body. The shrill mizmar is more energetic and is often used in the Saiidi—the Egyptian cane dance usually performed by men.

The Element of Water

Water is fluid, sensual and associated with the emotions. The flowing, undulating waves of sound produced by instruments like the accordion, saxophone and violin, entice the body to move in the same way. The melodies of such instruments, played close to the chest, are metaphorically described as 'sounds that pull the heart strings'. Snake-like undulations, figure-eights and swaying hips are the moves that respond to the water element. Water-element instruments usually produce a soulful, often melancholy sound. Earlier this century, the traditional rababa was replaced with various modern European orchestral instruments and the festive bellydance of old became more theatrical. Egyptian dance music became richer and more emotionally charged when the saxophone and accordion became the leading baladi instruments mid-century.

The stringed instruments from the chordophone family impart a fiery quality—passionate, warm and feisty. Spanish flamenco has a strong fire element because of the significance of the guitar. The strumming of the oud, saz, bazouki or qanoon can produce a tremolando effect that gives a confident energy to the dancer's moves. Played lower on the body, the strumming of the stringed instruments suggests an outward 'releasing' motion from the hips, with the arms in a lower position than for the air-element instruments. A dynamism and sense of desire accompany the fervour of the guitars—electric or acoustic. The element of fire opens the body for outward movements: turns, sweeping gestures and soft shimmies that last as long as the tremolando strumming does. Through the cello and bass, the element of fire breathes energy, depth and passion into bellydance music.

The Element of Earth

Drums and percussion are earthy, and the heavier, more robust and closer to the ground, the lower the response in the body. African music, for example, is very earthy because of its emphasis on drums. The drums set the pace of the music and the dancer must listen to the repetitive patterns they create. The steady backbone rhythm of the doholla or tambour sets the pulse for the stepping of the feet; the weight changes from right to left with the heaviness of the move matching that of the music. The darbuka or tabla rhythm, played higher, near the hips, synchronises the rhythmic patterns of the dancer's hip movements, from hip drops and lifts to staccato accents and shimmies.

The lighter percussion instruments, played higher still, near the shoulders—like the reque or dof—can activate shoulder and upper body accents and shimmies.

When the percussion section plays a call-and-response, where different instruments take turns in 'talking', the dancer lends accent to the corresponding parts of her body accordingly. The tabla, for instance, may be calling the reque, so the dancer responds first with her hips, then with her shoulders. Although this call-and-response occurs intermittently throughout a routine, it is normally placed with the exciting finale or drum solo. And even shimmies can have character! The nuance within the rolling darbuka shimmy can be interpreted in different ways by the dancer. She can raise and lower the level of her hips by bending her knees in response to the depth of the sound. The tonal depth depends on the part of the darbuka skin being played—a higher sound when the edge is used, to create the shimmy, and a lower, bass tone when the centre is struck, perhaps accentuated by a hip thrust or drop.

5

RHYTHM

The way the percussion is played sets the rhythm of the music. The rhythm is the pattern and arrangements of beats and accents—the backbone of the composition. The tempo is the timing or speed of the rhythm.

A darbuka is played by striking the skin with an open hand or with the fingers. The bass note created by striking closer to the centre of the drum is called a 'dom'. It is heavy and suits a flat or downward step of the feet or movement of the hips. The treble note is the 'tak', struck on the rim to produce a higher, sharper accented sound. There is also an even sharper sound that drummers in the West call a 'cut', which is more abrupt than a tak. However, for simplicity, we will only focus on the bass and treble beats.

When this series of doms and taks is arranged in specific ways, the rhythms are formed. A popular Egyptian rhythm is known in the West as 'the baladi rhythm', although, technically speaking, there are many baladi rhythms. This particular rhythm, however, is the best known and its beat pattern is as follows:

dom-dom tak-a-tak,
dom tak-a-tak

The front-heaviness of the two doms in the first half is good for hip drops, as it has a downward pull, and also for a step-point. The flat step follows the doms and the pointed step is executed on the taks. The dancer matches the pattern: bass, treble, bass, treble. An opportune time for turning would be during a tak, when the foot is lifted off the ground.

Another similar baladi rhythm is the maqsoum, with a faster, simpler structure than the above.

Egyptian rhythms are heavier and consist of more doms than Turkish rhythms. This shows in the way the dances vary. Egyptian dance is more grounded and uses the characteristic hip drop, whereas Turkish dance is full of hip lifts. A popular Turkish and Greek rhythm, the chiftetelli, has quite a different sound pattern:

dom-tak-tak, tak-tak
dom-dom tak

It is middle-heavy and is good for stationary, round and deep hip moves like hip circles and figure-eights. The travelling movement it produces is rather 'slinky' compared with the vibrant, repetitive Egyptian maqsoum, which is fun to dance a lively step to.

A Saiidi rhythm gives the stylised cane dance of the Saiidi warriors its forward-back reeling motion:

dom-tak, dom-dom tak

The dom-tak produces a step-lift, yet the double dom-dom pulls the dancer back just as quickly. Hence the slow, exaggerated hopping of the Saiidi style.

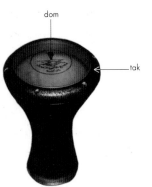

dom

tak

A malfuf entry rhythm with its repetitive and sprightly 'dom, tak-tak, dom, tak-tak' makes a rhythm that is perfect for a gliding triple step, and the heavy zaar's 'dom, a-tak-a, dom, a-tak-a' fuels the heavy, deep swaying of the trance dance.

Most Middle Eastern rhythms are played in four-four time, but there are plenty of variations. Usually, the dancer changes when the drummer does, after every set of four. This is commonly known as 'the rule of four', and helps immensely when improvising a dance or when choreographing a piece of music.

The following are some useful rhythms. Speak

them aloud as you read them. Note that the 'D' represents the dom; and the 't' represents the tak; a 'tkt' represents the faster series of taks that sounds like tak-a-tak; and ~ represents a pause or space. The 'tk' is vocalised as tak-a and the lengthier 'tktktk' sounds like a constant tak-a-tak-atak-a. The rhythms are illustrated in their simplest forms, without the many nuances a professional percussionist would add.

Egyptian

Malfuf (2/4)—A gliding entry and exit rhythm, good for triple steps. Made up of one dom and two rapidly following taks, it produces a light, flowing feel.
D t~t, D t~t

Maqsoum (4/4)—A basic baladi rhythm, good for lively stepping. It is one of the most frequently used Egyptian baladi rhythms.
DD~tD t, DD~tD t

Baladi (8/4)—A commonly used Egyptian-style drumming pattern in the West, describes one particular mode of a variety of popular Egyptian dance rhythms. It is included here because so many drummers call this regular, front-heavy pattern 'the baladi rhythm'. It is earthy and ideal for stepping moves and hip drops.
DD tkt Dtkt tk, DD tkt Dtkt tk

Masmoudi (8/4)—A characteristic rhythm of two distinct parts. The heavy doms in the first part of the rhythm can be played in groups of two or three. There are many ways of playing this rhythm; the doms can either be played closely or spaciously.
D D ~ t D ~ t t, D D ~ t D ~ t t
D D D t D ~ t t, D D D t D ~ t t

Wahda l'kabira (8/4)—Meaning the 'big one', is a sensual rhythm with a similar feel to the chiftetelli. The simple accents give the drummer plenty of time to improvise within the rhythm. It often accompanies taqsim.

D ~ t t D D t ~, D ~ t t D D t ~

Fellahi (2/2)—A fast, repetitive rhythm, like a speedier version of the maqsoum, suited to hip lifts and shimmy walks.

Dtk Dt, Dtk Dt

Zaar (2/4)—A religious trance dance where the head is flicked from side to side as the upper body sways.

D~tDt, D~tDt

Saiidi (4/4)—The rhythm for the masculine cane dance of upper Egypt, danced with a forward-back reeling motion. The Saiidi is sometimes referred to as the 'Ghawazee rhythm' from the dance of gypsies who settled in Egypt, as the two rhythms are very similar.

D t~ DD t, D t ~ DD t

Bambi (4/4)—A baladi rhythm similar to the wahda l'kabira, characterised by three doms. However, bambi is usually played faster, so that the three doms are close together.

DDD tktktkt, DDD tktktkt

Zaffa (8/4)—A traditional rhythm that accompanies a wedding procession.

Dtt t t D t t ~, Dtt t t D t t~

Chiftetelli (8/4)—A sensual rhythm used in Greek and Turkish music, associated with the ancient 'dance of veils' that was practised in the temples of Artemis and Aphrodite. The pattern consists of eight parts, with a middle heaviness that suggests movements that are grounded and circular.
D tt tt D D t ~, D tt tt D D t ~

Karsilama (9/8)—A unique folk rhythm, also called the 'mastika', where dancers face each other. The heavy stepping is done on the first three doms, and twists on the toes for the three successive beats that constitute the last part of the rhythm. The ninth beat gives this rhythm an odd pause.
Dt Dt Dt Dtt, Dt Dt Dt Dtt

Lebanese

Many of these rhythms are the same as Egyptian rhythms.

Ayoub (2/4)—A heavy rhythm used in dabke folk dancing and is incorporated into modern Lebanese music nowadays.
D t~ DD ~, D t~ DD ~

Nawari (4/4)—A folkloric rhythm used in Lebanese line dances.
tD tkt D tkt, tD tkt D tk

Nubian

Jairk (4/4)—A modern Nubian rhythm, often used in Egyptian pop songs. It is played quite fast.
D t DD~t, D t DD~t

Arabian Gulf

Khaleegee   (2/4)—A rolling rhythm that is danced with a hopping step with one foot forward.

Dt~ Dtkt, Dt~ Dtkt

Persian

Darj   (6/8)—A sprightly six-beat rhythm that is played quickly. The last two beats can be left out, as pauses, or they can be filled in by the percussionist. Persian rhythms can be very complex—some are played with up to sixteen parts.

D tkt D t ~~, D tkt D t ~~

Persian   (2/3)—This simple Persian rhythm creates an asymmetrical rolling feel that can be counted quickly as 'one-two-three, one-two-three'.

D t t, D t t

Moroccan

Sha'bia   (6/8)—A foundational part of a Moroccan polyrhythm (blend of two or more rhythms). Moroccan rhythms are more complex than Egyptian or Turkish rhythms, as they are layered.

ttDt ttDt tt, ttDt ttDt tt

Moroccan   (6/8)—An earthy base for a simple polyrhythm, played with several other percussionists.

Dtt DtD ~, Dtt DtD ~

'ORIENTAL DANCE HAS A TRANCE-
LIKE QUALITY THAT COMES FROM
CONCENTRATION ON THE
RHYTHM, ON BEING TOTALLY
WITH IT, IN IT.'

BADIIYAA LEMNIAI,
MOROCCO

PART TWO

THE ART OF BELLYDANCE

6

BENEFITS

Bellydancing is both a relaxing and enlivening dance that can help tone the body and improve body confidence. Its physiological benefits include improved fitness, circulation and suppleness, and correction of postural alignment. On a body confidence level, many women feel they regain their feminine self and become more comfortable with their bodies through bellydancing. Bellydancing can be taken up at any age. I have had students begin at 75 and do their first performance within months! A wonderful and colourful activity for young and old, bellydancing is interesting in terms of variety of movements, music and cultural styles. Community classes are a good way to meet people and inspire a friendly, non-competitive environment for fitness.

The basis of the core moves in bellydance is always the centre—just below the navel—or, in esoteric arts, the place known as the hara, second charka or simply 'the centre'. Yoga and Pilates are two popular exercises that, like bellydancing, focus their energies on the centre and the breath, which are two key factors in building core abdominal strength, revitalising internal organs and improving posture and balance.

Physical fitness can greatly improve with regular sessions of bellydancing. It helps firm and tone the muscles in a gentle way, especially the abdominals, arms, upper back, hips and thighs. Bellydancing can be a fun and energetic form of aerobic dance; an upbeat bellydance 'workout' lasting for at least 30 minutes, practised three to four times a week, will certainly improve muscle tone and overall fitness. Working out to fast-paced, repetitious music with spicy tabla rhythms will make the exercise more enjoyable. A series of constant stepping moves, lifting and alternating arm poses and shimmies is the basis for a safe, low-impact workout. As with all safe aerobics practice it is advisable to begin with a warm-up consisting of gentle movements, in this case shoulder rolls, arm lifts, basic step-points and circular moves. Then gradually increase speed and repetition of moves, and after the workout remember to stretch and cool down.

The suppleness and fluidity of movement necessary for bellydancing can help relax and lubricate joints and can be helpful in cases of arthritis, particularly in the wrists and shoulders. The dance, practised gently in the beginning stages, usually produces beneficial results for muscle and joint conditioning. Participants who have suffered uncomfortable back pain or shoulder stiffness for years have reported improvement after a few weeks of bellydancing. It is becoming a popular form of rehabilitation exercise, often suggested by doctors and therapists. Of course, if anyone has chronic back or knee problems, they are advised to see a doctor first before embarking on a bellydance course.

The relaxing benefits of bellydancing calm the mind and assist the focus required to learn new movements. Repetitious swaying, circular and flowing movements are likened to a state of dance-meditation. A session of taqsim, or slow, graceful dancing, will often clear the mind and induce a state of mental relaxation. The faster forms of bellydance are stimulating and fun, and either slow or fast bellydancing can be useful in cases of anxiety or mild depression.

Body confidence

Bellydancing boosts self-esteem in a gentle yet powerful way. The movements are artistic and feminine, creating a positive feeling of sensual expression and freedom. With sensuality being a desirable quality of bellydancing, the dancer feels safe to explore the soft, beautiful ways the body can move. Sensual taqsim (slow circular dance) is emotively charged and deeply felt, inspired by the haunting melodies of the East. In Western societies bombarded with mixed messages about self-expression, many find this extremely liberating. In the act of dancing and exploring her own sensuality, the dancer frees herself in physical and emotional ways.

The body, which becomes increasingly supple and graceful through practising the dance, literally begins to move more beautifully. Dancers feel a heightened sense of elegance and poise when they dance, and this confidence remains long after a class or performance is finished.

The body awareness that comes from bellydancing often triggers an emotional response. Women begin to see and relate to their bodies differently: those with low self-image begin to honour their bodies; those who were previously weight-conscious participants relax and become comfortable with their belly and hips; and voluptuous women begin to appreciate their ample curves. In this light, bellydancing is possibly one of the most liberating arts, especially for women today.

As a bellydance teacher for over seventeen years, I have seen hundreds of incredible transformations in my students in terms of self-confidence and personal empowerment. Some treasured quotes I have gathered from students concerning their improved self-confidence and poise through bellydancing are:

'I can walk with more dignity—I feel like a queen!'

'After years of slouching I have finally lifted my shoulders and walk proudly.'

'My chest and heart have opened, I can love more.'

The strengthening effects of the earthy shimmies and grounded steps used in bellydance have an empowering effect too. They bring out a primal assertion in the body's expression—clear and confident. Some dancers have said:

'My feet are more earthed, I feel stronger.'

'The strength that bellydancing has given me has flowed into my personal life.'

'As I dance better, I communicate more clearly in relationships!'

Coordination, symmetry and spatial awareness are elements of bellydancing that help improve body confidence too. There's an exclamation I hear often (and smile every time I hear it):

'Since I've started bellydancing I feel so much sexier!'

Bellydancing originated thousands of years ago as a fertility rite—the circular hip movements celebrating the birth process through mimicry. Similar movements can be seen in other dances that have evolved from birth-rites and celebrations of sexuality and fertility such as Hawaiian hula, Polynesian dance, African dance, Brazilian samba and Latin lambada. Often associated with religious rites and celebrations, the primal elements of both divinity and sexuality are central to the evolution of these forms of dance.

Today, bellydance is linked with birthing mainly through its focus on the belly and hips. As a pre-natal exercise, bellydancing in its gentler form strengthens the pelvic muscles and relaxes the mother-to-be. Many Arab women say shimmies should be avoided during pregnancy, but the figure-eights and rolling circular movements are good preparation for childbirth. This makes sense, as the rolling movements not only feel natural but assist with the normal pelvic relaxing process to prepare for birth and, at the same time, help firm the pelvic muscles for labour and post-pregnancy recovery. Indeed, the dance can be a comfortable exercise that not only gets the mother ready for the birth process, but connects her to the unborn child through a series of movements that focus her attention on her belly.

Midwives in the Middle East report that Bedouin women often give birth in a tent with the elders present and several women playing tabla and breathing in unison with the mother. The communal drum beat and vocalised breathing become part of the birth-dance process. The mother, supported by two other women, does not lie down but rather alternates between standing and squatting, and uses hip circles and rolling motions to ease the baby into the world. Nowadays, Western doctors are also advising women to incorporate gentle bellydancing into their pre-natal and post-natal activities. I have had several gynaecologists and countless midwives in my classes—all long-time students who recommend bellydancing in pregnancy and promote it in their own practices.

Pregnant mothers find that bellydancing helps relieve back pain and keeps the body supple. Many of my students who were second-time mothers after taking up bellydancing reported much easier, more relaxed births with the 'bellydance baby'. The body also gets into shape quickly, the pelvic floor muscles are toned and strengthened, thereby improving problems with incontinence and the general condition of health is better with regular dancing sessions. Mothers in my classes have also reported that their babies often like swaying in their arms when they're doing figure-eights and dancing to soft music!

Bellydancing and childbirth have been inextricably linked for thousands of years— from the days of ancient female deity worship to tribal fertility ceremony, harems and existing birthing customs in Arabian villages. Celebrating the miracle of birth with its original dance reflects gratuity and praise for the creation of life.

Menstruation

Menstruation comes from the Latin term 'menses' which means monthly. The lunar month of approximately 29 days is also the approximate cyclic timing of the menstrual cycle. In ancient times, the lunar cycle and a woman's menses were seen to be divinely linked, as recorded in the ancient cult of Artemis (or Diana, Huntress of the Moon), which existed in Ephesus near what is now the town of Selcuk in Turkey.

Artemisian legend, steeped in ritualistic, matriarchal religion, tells that the woman's period fell on the dark moon and that, conversely, ovulation occurred on the full moon. The priestesses and dancers of the Temple of Artemis would dance ecstatically on the four mountain tops of Ephesus at the time of the full moon—to worship their deity and to celebrate with the men folk! The dance they did was called the chiftetelli—full of wild shimmies and abandoned movements danced as a fertility rite. This, they knew, was most likely the time for conception, and the dance became frenzied and trance-like with a communal, ritualistic sexual fervour. However, at the time of the dark moon, the dancers would sway gently, alone and quietly, rolling their hips in a meditative contemplation.

Gentle bellydance is a relaxing way to stimulate the blood flow and, for some women, a way to tune into and enjoy their periods. The problem of PMS, or pre-menstrual syndrome, affects many young women in their childbearing years. Physical and emotional blockages can contribute to the painful condition—and stress only serves to make the problem worse. However, soothing bellydance movements such as rolling the hips, figure-eights and undulations can help alleviate congestion in the pelvic area, and as a result, improve circulation, and the relaxation of body and mind helps to alleviate stress.

My students have reported over the years that one of the most incredible benefits of bellydancing has been the relief of PMS, which some suffered from quite severely. As a teenager, I too had chronic PMS but, thanks to bellydancing, I have never again had to deal with painful periods. For anyone experiencing this monthly discomfort in the days leading up to their period, relaxed, slow bellydancing can be beneficial in the reduction of pain and pelvic congestion. Practising a deep belly breath whilst dancing is also helpful. Breathing, remaining calm and focusing on the moves is a wonderful 'active meditation' which is mentally and physically soothing.

7

BASIC WARM-UP EXERCISES

It is important to warm up before you begin practising your bellydance movements, and just as important to stretch the muscles when you finish, with a cool-down. These simple exercises can be done before and after your practice sessions. Wear comfortable clothing like leotards and tights, with a scarf around the hips to accentuate movement in that area. Walking on the spot for five minutes to your favourite tune will gently loosen the muscles before you begin the following exercises. As with any form of physical activity, it is a good idea to consult your doctor beforehand if you are pregnant or have any existing injuries.

Before you start

1. Posture and alignment: Suppleness and flexibility are required for bellydancing, so warm-ups and correct posture are paramount. The posture is very balanced—stand with feet flat, slightly apart, knees soft and thighs strong. Feel your weight transfer gently from foot to foot, with a rocking movement in the pelvis. Tilt the pelvis upwards, so that your bottom tucks under. Align the pelvic centre of gravity with the feet. Then relax and expand your torso area by lifting the chest and relaxing the shoulders. Align the centre of gravity in the chest and shoulders with the pelvis and feet. Next, lift the head and align the head and neck with the rest of the body. The posture should be comfortable, fully aligned and grounded.

2. Breathing: Breathing is very important in bellydancing technique, as the moves flow smoothly when the breath flows freely. Avoid holding your breath at any time, particularly when concentrating on a new movement. A good breathing exercise to do, when in the correct posture, is to place the hands low on the belly with the fingertips just touching. Take a slow, deep breath through the nose and draw the breath into the belly, feeling your lower abdominal area expanding with the full breath. The fingertips should move apart. Remember not to raise your shoulders. Exhale fully, slowly releasing the air through the mouth, feeling the belly return to its normal position. Then do this exercise in two distinct stages—first, as before, breathe in and expand the belly, then continue this breath expansion into the chest and back. The rib cage expands, yet the shoulders stay relaxed. Then exhale, with the chest returning to normal, followed by the belly.

3. Arm extension: Lift the arms outwards and up over your head as you inhale, then exhale fully with a flowing movement downwards.

4. Side extension: Take one leg out to the side, pointing your toe and extending your arm outwards as you inhale. Bring your arm and leg back to resting position as you exhale. Repeat with the other leg. Then repeat the sequence several times, in a flowing, graceful manner.

5. Back stretch: Stand with feet wide apart and bend your knees, squatting slightly, but keeping your back straight, similar to a horse-riding position. Tuck your pelvis upwards, then release it, repeating several times.

6. Thigh stretch: From the previous position (the back stretch), stretch to one side, straightening one leg and leaning over the other bent knee to stretch your thigh

De-Rosario

muscles. Hold for ten seconds, breathing normally, and repeat with the other leg. Come up slowly, returning to the correct posture.

7.   Arm stretch: Stretch upwards with your arms, taking one elbow in the opposite hand and gently stretch your arm behind your head. Repeat on the other side.

8.   Hip stretch: Return to the basic postural alignment position. Slowly, press your weight from one foot to the other, keeping the knees soft and the chest relatively still and centred. This begins to stretch the hips. Step from side to side for a few minutes, using your arms as in the arm extension, to limber up the body in preparation to performing isolations, before beginning to dance.

UPPER BODY ISOLATIONS

Choose music with a slow, steady tempo or a rhythm like the masmoudi, wahda l'kabira or chiftetelli.

Shoulders

Shoulder roll—A supple alternating roll of the shoulders with graceful arms. Stand with one foot slightly behind you and draw a circle with your right shoulder by gently pressing the shoulder forwards, rolling it up towards the ear—without hunching the shoulders—pressing it back, then pressing it downwards. Repeat several times, then repeat with the left shoulder. Next, begin rolling shoulders smoothly in an alternating fashion, i.e. when one shoulder is up, the other is down and vice versa. Bring some graceful energy into the arms and hands by becoming aware of neat, flowing hands, with fingers lengthened.

Shoulder accent—Press alternate shoulders forwards and backwards, keeping your chest still and arms out to the sides, with palms down. Resist moving anything but your shoulders. It is a strong, sharp move.

Shoulder shimmy—Increase the speed of the previous shoulder accents, until you have a fast, smooth and relaxed shoulder shimmy.

Shoulder routine
- four shoulder rolls
- four shoulder accents
- four shoulder rolls
- four shoulder shimmies

SHOULDER SHIMMY   SHOULDER ROUTINE

Arms

Classic arms—Hold out your arms in front of you and whilst rolling your shoulders, alternate the arm levels in a sinewy, graceful manner. This move looks best when the body is turned to the side.

Snake arms—Similar to classic arms, except the arms are held out, extended from the sides of the body. While one shoulder, elbow and hand are up, the other arm is down. In a slow, smooth transition, alternate arm positions. Repeated slowly and sensuously, with relaxed shoulders, it is a beautiful move.

Arm routine
- eight classic arms
- eight snake arms

SNAKE ARMS

Hands and wrists

Hand position—Graceful, elongated. To achieve an elegant, relaxed look, keep the fingers close together, with the index and little finger slightly higher, and the middle finger slightly lower. Resist splaying the fingers. Aim for a soft flow of the hand when the melody is flowing, and a neat position when framing a sharp, accented move.

Wrist roll—A smooth, flexible circular motion of the hands from the wrists. The gesture is an inward scooping motion, with the fingers flowing softly. As you use your hand, the tip of your thumb faces the tip of your middle finger, with about 3–4 centimetres of space in between them. Lift your index finger and little finger slightly higher than the rest.

Snake wrist—With the same basic hand position, bring your bent arm in front of you, palm facing downwards, elbow up. Keeping the arm quite still, let the hand flow, joint by joint, like a snake moving on the ground. This move looks nice when passing across the face, under the eyes.

Hand and wrist routine
- four wrist rolls with arms extended outward, slowly lifting up over head
- four wrist rolls with arms crossing in the front and moving downwards, in front of face, under the eyes
- four snake wrists with arms moving outwards, until arms are wide open
- four snake arms

Head

Head slide—A sideways slide of the head, face forwards, without turning or tilting it. Using the muscles behind the neck, slide your head to the left, then to the right. It is a difficult move to master. However, the main objective is to keep your head on a level plane and not to bring the side of your head down to your shoulders. The move is best framed with hands crossing in front, at your neck, or crossing above your head.

HEAD SLIDE

MIDDLE BODY ISOLATIONS

Some of these movements involve the whole of the middle body, as with the undulations. Others isolate the rib cage or the abdominals.

Rib cage

Rib cage roll—A smooth circle drawn with the rib cage isolated from the rest of the body. It begins as a slide from right to left with the rib cage only. The next step is to trace the outline of a horizontal circle—like using a hula hoop—with the upper body, without moving either the shoulders or hips. The circular motion can be quite small and still look very effective.

Torso

Undulations—There are several styles of undulations, all serpentine and flowing. The undulation is a controlled forward and backward rocking motion of the body. Place one foot behind you and push your chest forwards, keeping the rest of your body still while transferring your weight to your front foot. Slowly pull in your abdominal muscles, so that your pelvis rolls upwards and your chest goes back as your weight is transferred to your back foot. Continue this slow, muscular movement until an easy flow is achieved. Remember, it takes time and patience to achieve a smooth undulation.

Belly roll—An even more concentrated muscular move with an undulating quality. Push your belly outwards, using the abdominal muscles only, not the spine. Then begin to pull in from

ZØ5Ø55 // PR0T0.TYPE

◄2

◄3

BELLY ROLL

the upper abdominals, using the muscles surrounding the diaphragm area. Next, isolate the middle belly (behind the navel), bearing down so the roll appears to be 'travelling' downwards. Lastly, bring the lower abdominals inwards, using the pelvic floor muscles to pull in your lower belly. Release again and continue this rolling motion. It really firms your belly!

Hip undulation—A similar move to the full torso undulation, except the chest is kept still and the movement is contained in the hip and belly area.

Middle body routine
- four slow hip undulations
- four slow rib cage rolls
- four slow full torso undulations
- four slow belly rolls

10

LOWER BODY ISOLATIONS

Play a slow, rhythmic piece of music or percussion to practise these hip movements. Keep them simple and slow, concentrating on posture, the shift of weight, strength in the thighs and softness in the knees. Frame the moves with your hands.

Hip circles—Standing with feet slightly apart, trace a small, horizontal circle with your hips. With soft knees and strong, yet relaxed leg muscles, you should experience the weight change around the soles of your feet as you draw the circle—the weight goes from the ball of the right foot to the heel, then to the heel of the left foot to the ball, etc. Keep your chest still.

Pelvic roll—A concentrated version of the hip circle, where the pelvis is smoothly tucked inwards during the frontal section of the circular movement, by engaging the abdominal muscles.

Outward figure-eights—Imagine a number eight on the floor, one foot in each half. Begin to trace this eight with your hips by pushing your hips diagonally to the right, weight in the ball of your right foot. Slowly continue tracing the eight by pushing your hips backwards, weight shifting to your right heel. Then continue, diagonally tracing the left side as before, from front to back, weight changing from the ball of your foot to the heel. The aim is a smooth, flowing figure of eight—a gentle sway of the hips, driven by the strength in the thighs and the relaxation of the knees, while the feet are kept flat.

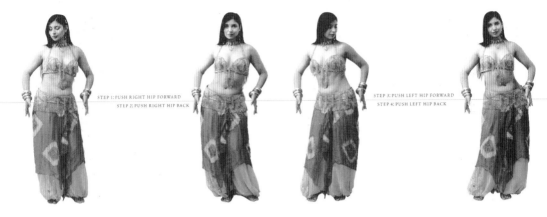

STEP 1: PUSH RIGHT HIP FORWARD
STEP 2: PUSH RIGHT HIP BACK

STEP 3: PUSH LEFT HIP FORWARD
STEP 4: PUSH LEFT HIP BACK

First hip routine
- four hip circles clockwise
- four hip undulations
- four outward figure-eights
- four hip circles anticlockwise

Inward figure-eights—To twist the hips from back to front, you must first take the weight of the move in the right heel. Moving your heel off the ground, slowly twist your weight into the front of your foot, turning your foot and hip inwards. Then transfer your weight from the ball of your right foot to the heel of your left foot, before turning the ball of your left foot and hip inwards again. When the movement gains momentum, you feel your hips gently twisting inwards from the lower torso, heels lifting off the floor.

Maya—A vertical outward figure of eight likened to 'honey spilling over the edge of a cup'. Your knees must be bent more than for the other styles of figure-eights to allow for a vertical movement and extension in the hips. First, standing with feet slightly apart and

STEP 1: LIFT RIGHT HIP, STRAIGHTEN
RIGHT LEG

STEP 2: DROP RIGHT HIP AND
TRANSFER WEIGHT TO LEFT SIDE

STEP 3: LIFT LEFT HIP

STEP 4: DROP LEFT HIP

knees softly bent, lift your right hip upwards, outwards to the right and then downwards—transferring your weight into your right foot. As the right hip moves down vertically, the left hip rises upwards, then takes its turn to move outwards and down. The vertical 'eight' continues like this. Aim to keep your feet flat and to really extend your hips. This is a more advanced move which takes practice.

Vertical inward figure-eights—The opposite to maya, the vertical hip figure-eight rolls inwards, always returning to the centre. This move is concentrated and looks best when the level of the move changes by bending the knees, allowing for an up-and-down motion in the body.

Second hip routine
- four inward figure-eights
- four faster vertical inward figure-eights, up and down
- four outward figure-eights
- four maya outward or vertical figure-eights

11

HIP ACCENTS AND SHIMMIES

For accents, choose a steady rhythm like baladi. For the shimmies, work with an Egyptian fellahi rhythm or a fast drum solo.

The accents

Hip drop—A typically Egyptian move, where the hip moves from a raised position to a deep-seated one. Stand with your feet fairly close, right foot slightly in front. Lift the right foot a little, so that your weight rests on the back foot. Keep your knees soft and lift your right hip upwards. In a strong accented motion, drop your right hip downwards, without moving your upper body. One heavy drop and one lighter 'half drop' are repeated in sequence. A small kick can be created by lifting your foot off the floor on the half drop.

Wahda wa noss—Accented hip drops. The term literally means 'one and a half'. This move is performed to an Egyptian baladi rhythm by following the rhythmic structure. The first hip drop is performed in two stages, dropped halfway and then fully, lifted, and followed by the heavier single hip drop. Or it can be changed around to suit the particular rhythm. A Saiidi rhythm, for example, would suit a hip drop, followed by a quick lift, then immediately followed with a hip drop in two stages.

Hip lift—Quick raising of the hip. This movement is used frequently in Turkish and Lebanese dance, though it also appears in Egyptian dance. It is the opposite of the hip drop. Less

HIP LIFT HIP DROP

grounded and more exuberant, the lift raises the leg and hip upwards and outwards in a strong accented movement. Again, refrain from moving the upper body.

Hip thrust—A dynamic accent to the side, where the hip pushes outwards and all the weight transfers from one foot to the other. Imagine you have your arms full of groceries and you need to shut the car door with your hip!

Hip accents routine
- four hip drops on right
- four hip drops on left
- four hip drops on right
- four thrusts—right, left, right, left
- Repeat routine starting on left side

HIP THRUST LEFT   HIP THRUST RIGHT

Pelvic tuck—Similar to a hip lift, but the movement is more centred and the abdominal muscles tuck the pelvis upwards. A single tuck can make a good accent. This movement is often used in Turkish bellydance.

Pelvic release—The opposite to a tuck. It is a move the Egyptian and Lebanese dancers frequently use as accents. The abdominal muscles suddenly release the hips and belly forwards and down in a sharp accented move. It is best done with one foot slightly in front of the other and a downward movement of the ball of the front foot when the hips shift back.

The shimmies

Hip shimmy—A vibration through knees and thighs to hips. Stand with your feet slightly apart, feeling very grounded with strong thighs and soft knees. Begin to tremble your knees and thighs backwards and forwards, creating a vibrating momentum throughout the fleshy part of the inner thighs and bottom. This shimmy vibrates through the hips, yet the energy is quite contained in the lower body. Keep your feet flat, relax and loosen the lower body for the shimmy, without moving the upper body.

Transfer shimmy—A basic shimmy, that shifts from side to side. Starting with equal weight on both feet and the feet flat, transfer the shimmy from one hip to the other by changing weight in the feet. However, it is important that the rest of your body is kept still and straight, so it looks like your hips are moving in isolation.

Layered shimmies—Can be achieved with practice. They are a blend of two moves—the vibrating shimmy, together with a smooth figure-eight, undulation or circle movement with the hips.

12

WALKS AND TRAVELLING STEPS

The styles of locomotion used in bellydance vary from a light glide to an earthy, grounded step. There are many ways of travelling while you dance, but the continuous flow and ease of movement is just as important as being in time with the rhythm.

Here are some basic steps that you can put together in sequence later. Focus on footwork first, and then when it feels comfortable and does not require all your concentration, frame the movement with your arms. Also, remember the 'rule of four'(p 24).

Triple step—A smooth, continuous gliding step that resembles the quick cha-cha-cha in Latin dance. Leading with the right foot first, transfer your weight from right, left, right (on the spot), to left, right, left. Keep changing the leading foot as you perform this gliding step. You can count the 'one, two, three, change, one, two, three, change,' etc. The transferral of weight from the front foot to the back foot, and vice versa, adds lightness and spring to the step. It suits an entry or exit, usually to the malfuf rhythm, where the dancer can create a sweeping circle around the stage or room. The arms sweep outwards, opening towards the leading leg and hip.

Triple step backwards—The same as the forward triple step, except your leading foot is the one you step back on. This step, though, works best in fours, with the dancer facing forwards.

Triple step routine

- four triple steps forwards, arms up
- four triple steps backwards, arms pointing out and forwards at head height, synchronising with the leading foot.

Step-point—A grounded movement, where the dancer steps flat with the right foot and points out with the left toe. Then she steps flat with the left foot and points out with the right toe. This pattern is continued. In folkloric dance, the flat step usually corresponds to the dom or bass beat in the rhythm. However, in classical cabaret-style dance, this is reversed: the toe points out on the dom beat and as the leg straightens, the hip thrusts forwards, creating a subtle accent. The arms usually move outwards with the toe pointing out, either at hip height or head height, resting at the temple or behind the ear. This step works well with the baladi rhythm.

Step-point routine
- four step-points forwards, arms pointing out from hip
- four step-points backwards, arms pointing out from head

STEP-POINT

The camel walk—A travelling undulation to the side, body facing the front, with one foot continuously leading. It can be performed on the balls of the feet, as this gives the legs a chance to bend and change in level as the undulation takes place. There are two ways of performing a camel walk: either with the entire torso undulating, from ribs to pelvis, or with the hips undulating alone. The movement feels like a smooth rocking motion, back and forth, with the weight shifting from foot to foot. When it is time to change direction, lead with the other foot. The arms open out to the direction of the move.

Camel walk routine
- four camel walks to the right
- four camel walks to the left

Split-level camel walk—Includes alternating the step of the leading foot continually, from flat to raised, making the undulations look even more effective. The aim is to keep the chest fairly still and rock from the hips, using your knees and thighs to alternate your level. This walk is often done in double time.

Split-level camel walk routine
- four double-time split-level camel walks (i.e. up and down) to the right
- four double-time split-level camel walks (i.e. up and down) to the left

Combination travelling routine (use baladi rhythm with strong drums)
- four step-points forwards, arms alternately pointing at hip height, synchronising with leading foot
- four triple steps backwards, arms alternately pointing out at hip height, synchronising with leading foot

- two regular camel walks, with two double-time split-level camel walks to the right
- two regular camel walks, with two double-time split-level camel walks to the left

The Egyptian hip-down walk—A traditional baladi walk where the feet simply step one in front of the other. However, the art of this walk is to be able to lower the leading hip downwards with each step. To do this, maintain the correct posture and as you step forwards and down, step onto a flat foot. Physically lower the front hip. Then change. The arms are best framing this move at the hips, or slightly bent, extended out in front of you. This step suits the fast fellahi rhythm.

The shimmy walk—A traditional walk often used in Egyptian baladi. It takes a while to master, and it should appear effortless. First you must be able to shimmy smoothly, with the flesh on the thighs and hips reverberating softly. Then you must be able to do the Egyptian hip-down walk. Now, put the two together, shimmying as you walk. It works best when you walk straight forwards, or to the sides with the body facing the front. This step also suits the fast fellahi rhythm, especially when there is a tabla shimmy embellishing the rhythm.

PART THREE

ROUTINES AND TECHNIQUES

13

CHOREOGRAPHY AND IMPROVISATION

Learning a choreographed dance from a teacher, and working on it step by step, can help the new bellydance student understand how a series of movements are linked together and to match appropriate moves to the music. Whilst choreography can create a feeling of safety through its methodology, especially in group dances that are performed in unison (perhaps on stage), the ultimate aim for a dancer should be to learn how to use choreography to help her improvise. On the positive side, choreographed steps look neat because they are usually rehearsed to perfection and can make a dancer look polished. Knowing the steps have been designed to fit the musical piece gives a feeling of confidence. However, the negative aspects of over-choreographed work become apparent when you see how responsive improvised Middle Eastern dancing can be.

Successful improvisation is developed through a basic understanding of music, rhythm and transitions. Improvisation shows that a dancer feels confident enough to 'let the music guide her'. The routines of many famous bellydancers are a combination of choreography and improvisation.

Once the solo dancer knows the steps that suit the music, she allows herself some freedom of expression. She can respond to audience feedback, a humorous moment or a taqsim piece. Strict adherence to a rigidly set group of moves can hamper the dancer's spontaneity. If the mind is overly focused on dance technique, the dancer's technical 'left brain' takes precedence over the emotive 'right brain'. Concentrating on steps, turns and tricky transitions for an entire routine can impair the dancer's involvement with the music and dull her playfulness and sense of enjoyment.

Improvisation can still be reinforced with rudimentary choreographic techniques like the basic 'rule of four' (p 24). As this usually applies to most Middle Eastern musical compositions, movements and steps can be performed with more freedom.

Earlier in this book, I explained the fundamentals of musical interpretation. Knowing the music and rhythm—the raw material you will be working with—helps you to understand what you are listening for, and which part of the body will usually respond. On the following pages, I describe transitions and turns—the intermediary steps that create full, flowing movement to music. Also, there are some simple sixteen-part routines, grouping basic moves together. These routines, which I call A–Z bellydance routines, or parts of them, can be used in many different dances. Remember—know your music, practise your movements and learn how to link them with ease. Then let the music take over and . . . improvise!

14

TURNS AND TRANSITIONS

Once you have practised the individual moves used in bellydancing, you will want to be able to link them together smoothly and gracefully. Previously, we described some basic combinations to help you put groups of movements together. Now, we will look at transitory steps.

An easy way to remember when to change from one move to another is to change with the music. Usually, when the rhythm changes, the dancer's foot and hip work changes. Arm and body movements, however, tend to relate more closely to changes in melody. An easy way to adapt to respond to rhythmic change is to learn how to turn your body around on the beat and to change feet with minimal fuss.

THREE-STEP TURN

Three-step turn—A common turn comprised of three steps, taken to the side, as you turn. You use the fourth beat to stabilise the turn. To turn right, for example, you prepare by keeping your left foot flat and right toe pointed. You then turn clockwise as you step onto the right foot, then left foot, then right foot, which finishes flat. The left toe, pointing outwards, finishes and stabilises the move. The arms propel the movement by starting open, then 'hugging' inwards during the turn. As you come out of the turn, the arms release and open again, giving the movement a flowing elegance.

A tip for successful turning is to keep the body on an even level. Resist bobbing up and down, as it appears that you are losing your balance.

About-turn—Turning to face the opposite direction. As you perform a step-point move, you can turn your body around on the new 'step', after completing a series of fours. On the final 'point' the body is least grounded, and therefore is more capable of rotating. You can use this turn for a smooth continuation of movement when you want a set of moves to be viewed from both the front and the back.

Changing feet

Most transitions require either a change of weight in the feet or an actual step to commence a new move. Often, you can count into the rhythm if it is slow enough, 'one and two and three and four and . . .' As you count, the number denotes a flat step and the 'and' denotes a 'point' or transition from one foot to the other. A new move should begin on the 'one', so the transition is usually done after the fourth 'and'.

Sometimes you want to begin a move—a hip drop, for instance—on one hip, and then continue it on another. If you are doing double-time hip drops, Egyptian style, where one hip drop is lower than the next, you could call the lower, deep-seated drop 'deep' and the smaller hip drop 'light'. Then you would count 'one and two and three and four and . . .' or 'deep, light, deep, light, deep, light, deep, step back' and continue on the other hip. The 'step back' is simply a rapid change of the feet and placement of weight.

Another effective way of changing feet is to use a triple step, like a cha-cha-cha step in Latin or ballroom dancing. It transfers the weight to the opposite foot and therefore the movement can be repeated on the other side.

15

SIMPLE ROUTINES FOR BELLYDANCE

The following routines each consist of sixteen parts. One part can be counted as a 'step and a point' or as 'one and . . .' For example, when stepping forwards for four, count 'one and two and three and four and . . .' at a reasonably comfortable speed.

These routines help you to understand how to use various combinations of hip work and foot patterns, so that later you can dance to the music in an improvised way. The best rhythm to choose is a stepping-paced baladi, Saiidi or chiftetelli. Remember to focus on your footwork first, then add the arms. Another point to remember, so that you can smoothly join routines, is to always start with your right foot primed, i.e. left foot flat and right toe pointed, ready to go.

Routine A — 'Aswan'

- Four step-points forwards, i.e. start with flat right foot, left toe point, then flat left foot, right toe point, etc.
  (Arms pointing from the hips, straight out, always using the arm on the same side as the pointed foot)
- Four triple steps backwards
  (From a relaxed position, hands resting on the back of the head; arms point straight out, synchronising with the pointed foot)

- Four step-points in a full circle, clockwise
  (Shoulders shimmying)
- Four step-points in a full circle, anticlockwise
  (Shoulders shimmying)

Routine B — 'Bint al Balad'

(means 'the girl of the country')

- Four hip-rolling side steps to the right
  (Arms framing move, i.e. left up and right out to the side)
- Four hip-rolling side steps to the left
  (Arms framing move, i.e. right arm up and left arm out to the side)
- Four hip-rolling side steps; two to the right, two to the left, then turn the body around to face the back on the last beat
  (Have arms out at hip level and relaxed)
- Four hip-rolling side steps, facing the back; two to the right, two to the left, turn the body around to face the front on the last beat
  (Have arms out at hip level and relaxed)

Routine C — 'Cairo Cabaret'

- Four hip drops with the right hip
  (Arms framing move, i.e. left up and right out to the side)
- Step to the right foot, then left foot, turn to the right in three steps to two beats
  (Right foot should end up flat)
- Four hip drops with the left hip
  (Arms framing move, i.e. right up and left out to the side)
- Step to the left foot, then right foot, turn to the left in three steps to two beats
  (Left foot should end up flat)

Routine D — 'Delta'

- Step forwards on right foot, then back on left foot, then a triple step on the spot (right, left, right)

  (Left hand on left hip, right arm pointing out to right)

- Step forwards on left foot, then back on right foot, then a triple step on the spot (left, right, left)

  (Right hand on right hip, left arm pointing out to left)

- On last triple step, turn around and repeat both of these sequences again, then turn back to face the front on the second triple step

Routine E — 'Exotic Egyptian'

- Four hip rolls; two to the right side and two to the left side

  (Left hand low near left hip, right arm up, then change arms when you change direction)

- Figure of eight created by stepping onto right foot, then left foot.

- Two fast, double-time hip thrusts (right then left) and step back quickly to turn body (back on right foot and as you turn anticlockwise to face the back step on left, keeping left foot flat)

  (Arms out at waist level and relaxed)

- Repeat this entire sequence, facing the back

Routine F — 'Fellaha'

(means 'farm girl')

- Four triple steps forwards (Arms up)

- Four triple steps backwards (Arms pointing outwards from the head, straight out, synchronising with the pointed foot)

- Eight double-time hip thrusts to the right; four to the right and four turning clockwise on the spot

- Eight double-time hip thrusts to the left; four to the left and four turning anticlockwise on the spot

16

VEIL WORK

The veil has long been associated with the mystery of the Middle East. It conceals and reveals, serving as an aesthetic prop that enhances bellydancing. A rectangular or semicircular scarf made from approximately 2 metres of lightweight fabric like chiffon or organza, the veil adds an element of mystery when the dancer uses it for an entry piece, as it forms a sheer curtain between her and the audience. The veil can also embellish a movement of an arm or an undulation, framing the move, or softly falling as the move is being demonstrated. And, of course, there's nothing like the excitement generated by a wild, swirling veil that gives the dancer total command of the space she is dancing in.

Wrapping

The veil is initially tucked into the belt and then removed in several stages.

1.   Hold the veil out in front of you and tuck the left edge into your hip belt. Take the free short edge and hold the corners in both hands. Lift your arms high so the veil is hiding your body and face.

2.   Dance with slow movements. The silhouette looks mysterious behind the sheer veil. Spin.

3.   Slowly, bring the edge of the veil downwards, so your eyes are showing but your face is still covered.

4.   Turn. As you do, move your hands around the edges of the veil, getting closer to the hip. Take your right hand to where the left was, and then hold the first 20 centimetres

of the long edge under your eyes. Undulations and slow circles look lovely here.

5. Turn and slowly remove the veil from your hip belt in a neat and graceful way without tugging!

6. Now your veil is out and you can do some of the following veil techniques.

Veil techniques

- For mystery and concealment hold the veil in front of your body. Angle the veil diagonally and spin.

- Drape the veil to accentuate a movement. Highlight slow undulations, for instance, standing side-on with your back arm high and front arm low. Stop body movement and only lift your lower arm, drawing a big circle, veil flowing with this simple movement.

- Spin with the veil or do a three-step turn with graceful ease. Keep arms open. Spinning with the veil behind you while you do slow snake arms looks very elegant.

- For an impressive finale, there are several dramatic ways to shed the veil. You can begin by holding the outstretched veil in front of you, then throw the veil behind you as you briskly walk forward.

- A more subtle technique is to step out of a draped veil. Hold the veil in front of you, crossing your arms so the draped veil forms a gap. As you lift the veil in this position above your head, bring your arms behind your head and release the veil. It will fall into a neat pile on the floor so you can gracefully step over and out of it.

- Lastly, you can release the veil as you turn with it or twirl it in the air. However, this requires practice as the veil continues travelling on its own when thrown. Avoid getting tangled up in a wayward veil by aiming for a clear space, and releasing it half a turn earlier.

TAHLIA DEMONSTRATING THE STAGES OF THE VEIL TWIRL

Advanced techniques

Veil twirls—A continuous twirling motion of the veil over the head. Holding the long edge of the veil in front of you, gracefully take the veil behind you by lifting each arm above and around your head. It is easier if you lead with one arm and the other follows. Follow through to the front again. Repeat and build up speed until your arms are creating large circles and the veil is twirling briskly through the air.

Butterfly veil—A more advanced move where the veil is held out in front of you. Flick the left side over your left arm, still holding onto the veil, so the veil twists in the centre and looks like butterfly wings. Spin to the right. Then change arms by flicking the left side back to normal position and flicking the right side over your right arm. Spin to the left. Do this several times, remembering to keep the veil high up at shoulder level, briefly resting the veil on your shoulders as you spin with the 'wings'.

17

DANCING WITH THE STICK

The stick used most often in bellydancing is a bamboo cane with a hooked end. You can also use light wood like dowelling from a hardware store. It should be light enough to twirl between the fingers. You can decorate a stick, with gold tape and ribbon wrapped around the cane in a twisting pattern. The stick usually suggests Saiidi tradition, but Lebanese dancers also use sticks in their routines. The stick dance was once a folkloric dance art, where the costuming was a long dress and hip scarf, but these days, many dancers use it as part of a cabaret routine.

The first lesson in dancing with a stick is how to twirl it.

Twirling the stick

1. First, hold the stick at the non-hooked end, between the base of your thumb and the rest of the hand, resting it in the fleshy part of the hand between thumb and forefinger.
2. Hold the stick upwards, with the hooked end high in the air. Keeping the stick straight and parallel with your body, open your hand slightly, letting your palm face upwards as the stick falls down. You should be able to see the short, non-hooked end of the stick poking up between the base of your thumb and forefinger. You need only hold the stick loosely here.
3 Grasp the stick with the strength of your fingers to bring it back up to its original position.

4. Continue this release-grip-release-grip process, keeping the stick parallel with your body, to create a smooth twirl.

5. Now try this with a hip drop or hip lift.

Other popular stick moves

- Hold both ends of the stick in your hands at chest level as you shoulder shimmy.
- Hold both ends of the stick in your hands at hip level as you hip shimmy.
- Hold both ends of the stick in your hands at waist level as you rock your body forwards and backwards from right foot to left foot, keeping one foot in the front for the entire series of moves.
- Rest the hooked end of the stick on your shoulder.
- Hit the stick on the floor on an accented beat and bring it back up to your shoulder.
- Hit the stick on the floor on an accented beat and kick it with your foot to bring it back up to your shoulder.
- Hit the stick on the floor on an accented beat, then lift it over your head as you turn to the back, hitting the stick on the floor again. Then turn and bring it back up to your shoulder.
- Hold both ends of the stick in your hands at hip level as you do the travelling undulations.

Keep the movements strong and simple, and twirl the stick when the music gets especially festive. Egyptian baladi lends itself to the stick dance, with its earthy rhythms. For this, it would be best to wear a slim-fitting galebeya with a hip scarf and headscarf, lots of coin jewellery and small chin tattoos.

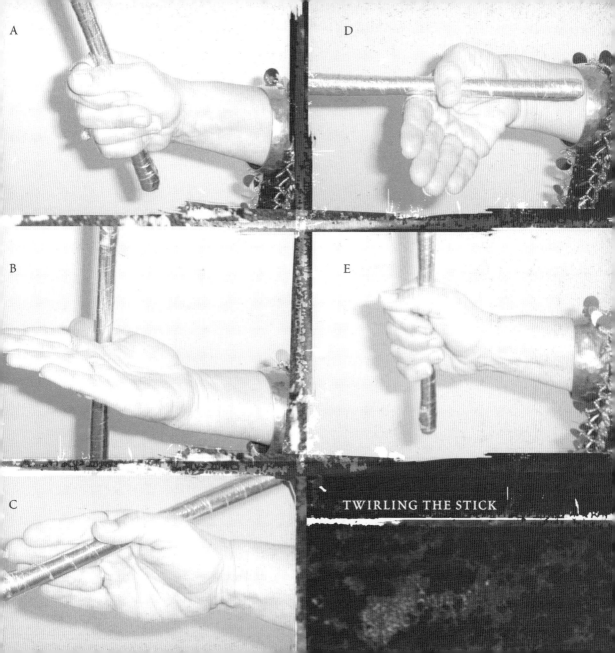

A

B

C

D

E

TWIRLING THE STICK

18

ZILLS (FINGER CYMBALS)

Brass finger cymbals played in Middle Eastern dance are known as 'zills' in Turkish and 'sagat' in Arabic. They are often played by dancers and sometimes by members of the band's percussion section or even by a group of women to announce the dancer's entry at festive events. They are intrinsic to folkloric styles of dance, yet are still used by modern bellydancers in all Middle Eastern countries. They are worn on the first joint of the middle finger and thumb of each hand, and are struck in alternating patterns to the music whilst dancing.

Since ancient times, bellydancers would play the finger cymbals for added excitement. The earliest metal finger cymbals were Egyptian, from Thebes, and soon became popular throughout the Middle East. Legend tells that the goddess Artemis was reputed to have used them while dancing a fast chiftetelli. Travelling gypsies were renowned for their metal crafts, from pots and pans to cymbals and drums, and gypsy dancers would herald their arrival into a village with zills. The Turks, too, have a history of manufacturing high quality brass cymbals. Their cymbals became especially ornate during the Ottoman era.

Zills are usually used to mark time, accompany and embellish the rhythm, and to enliven the dance. The 'chinking' sound of the finger cymbals varies from a light tinkering to a loud, brassy ringing. Zills made from a fine brass alloy resonate the best; the finer the quality, the prettier the sound. Middle Eastern marketplaces often sell cheap zills that sound flat or dull. This is due to the high lead percentage. Inferior zills look dull and their shape is irregular, whereas a quality zill is symmetrical and shiny. Elastic is threaded through the single or double hole at the top of the zill, and forms a firm-fitting ring around the fingers.

Thicker elastic, up to 1 centimetre in width, gives the dancer better control of the zills than thin, stringy elastic.

The best times to play zills

- To herald the dancer's arrival on stage and prepare the audience for a dynamic entrance.
- To sharpen the contrast of a set of lively moves after the dancer has removed her veil following a slow entrance.
- To engage in 'question and answer' dialogue with the percussion and music.
- To accompany the upbeat, folkloric section of a routine, adding an element of surprise.

Points to remember

- Less is more—don't play the zills unceasingly, they lose their appeal.
- Plan when in the routine you will play them for maximum effect.
- Don't be tempted to play them during taqsim sections. They are too lively.
- Do learn at least three rhythms for variety.
- Do play them when the music changes to lively and rapid.
- Resist playing them when you are shimmying.
- Play them when you are doing a fairly easy step so you don't get muddled.
- Feel free to be expressive, vocal and festive when you play the zills!
- Learn to lift your arms and change arm positions gracefully when playing the zills.
- When in doubt, leave zilling out!

Learning to play the zills whilst dancing takes patience. It is best to learn to play zill patterns first, seated, listening to music. You can play the patterns with whichever hand feels right and once you learn a few basic rhythmic patterns, embellish with faster playing in sections. Then, when you are ready, team the zill playing with simple steps.

Three easy patterns for finger cymbal playing
Simply follow the rhythms by striking the cymbal pairs on the right (r) or left (l) hand

Gallop—To a triple step, hip drops, hip circles or fast travelling 'camel walk' (undulation).
  rlr rlr rlr rlr

Baladi style—To a slow step-point or sideways-travelling figure-eight.
  r r rlr r rlr

Repetitive—To a fast hip lift or Egyptian walk.
  rlrlrlrlrlrlr

'WHY DO EGYPTIAN WOMEN DANCE? THE ANSWER IS

SURPRISINGLY SIMPLE. WHILE IN THE WEST WE LOOK FOR

A PROFOUND SIGNIFICANCE, THEY DANCE FOR NO OTHER

REASON THAN BECAUSE THEY ARE HAPPY AND WISH TO

EXPRESS THEIR JOY!'

LYNNELL, AUSTRALIA

PART FOUR

CULTURES AND DANCE

19

RAQS SHARQI

Throughout the Middle East today, the legacies of trade, cultural domination and artistic exchange have produced a more homogenous style of bellydance. Still highly expressive, this hybrid form of Middle Eastern dance has come to be known to both the Arab and Western worlds as oriental dance or 'dance of the East' as the Arabic name of *raqs sharqi* denotes. It is an accessible style that emerged at the turn of the century, crossing cultural boundaries. Chiefly an interpretive art, raqs sharqi is a melting pot of expressive oriental dance, drawing reference from sources as diverse as ballet, flamenco and classical Indian dance. It is an arena where classical, feminine styles of Egyptian dance meet dance moves from Ottoman Turkey, Persia and the Arabian Gulf.

Raqs sharqi has become a popular generic term in both the East and West for a relatively free and modernised form of bellydance. Being less constrained than the traditional dance forms, it is seen as closely resembling the cabaret style through which most Westerners first came to know Middle Eastern dance. In Egypt or Lebanon, for example, the cabaret bellydancer will be announced as 'a performer of raqs sharqi'. Certainly, the cabaret dancers that emerged during the period of a flourishing Middle Eastern cinema industry projected a very stylish, glamorous image inspired by the West. Hollywood starlets were emulated in an Eastern fashion. Hence the high-heeled shoes, brief costumes and glittering appeal of the actress/dancer. The raqs sharqi dancer often begins her routine with a long diaphanous veil, and often uses the many layers and fringing of her costume to emphasise her dramatic moves.

The raqs sharqi dancer does not limit herself to the cultural constraints of traditional Middle Eastern dance forms. Rather, she revels in the freedom of interpreting the music through a broad range of imaginative moves, steps and turns. Although traditional oriental movements are recognisable in this dance, it has become a performer's art—a dance with few structural rules and little stylisation. Within its broader and more general guidelines, it offers space for developing plenty of drama and sensitivity. It is a theatrical exploration of the endless possibilities of oriental-inspired dance.

Many dancers in the Middle East, especially Egypt and Lebanon, are exponents of the more recent sharqi style of dance. Even Nagua Fouad, one of the world's greatest Egyptian dance artists, who draws on traditional baladi, embellishes her oriental dance art with unique free-form moves. She has also trained for some time with a Turkish teacher. Today, Cairo's famous Dina has perfected her personalised art with a unique set of gestures that are hallmarks of her distinctive performance. She is particularly known for her exaggerated, staccato hip circle. A popular trend in Egyptian dance since the 1920s was for dancers to seek new and different artistic moves to make their dance unique. Dancers drew inspiration from many sources—Turkish floorwork, Vaudeville's fancy footwork and turns, and the Indian dancer's serpentine arms.

Baladi is a contained art, while sharqi is more outward in the sense that it seeks to elaborate the music rather than just to ride on it as baladi does. Whereas baladi is a more stylised, rhythmic dance form with the arms rarely extended from the body, raqs sharqi explores the fullest and most dramatic range of movement to interpret music. The sharqi artist is a performer. She enjoys the pleasure people derive from her expression and immersion in the music. Her art is to personify each instrument, every mood change, and constantly to transform the space that she fills.

20

SAIIDI EGYPTIAN STICK DANCE

El Saiid, which is upper Egypt, is most popular for its heavy rhythm. The 'Saiidi' that accompanies a dance of the same name, is performed with the stick or taktib. Resembling a martial art dance, the Saiidi was once used to train warriors for battle, as is evident in the tomb paintings depicting fighting scenes in ancient Egypt. Warriors would practise a series of gallant moves, steps, turns and lunges with the taktib, which was a large, heavy staff. The driving rhythm is played on the tabla, doholla and tambour, and is regularly accompanied by the mizmar (horn). The Saiidi rhythm fuels lunging, hopping and turning moves because of its structure: the first dom on the drum is followed by a sharp tak sound, creating a hop or release. The double dom in the middle of the rhythm pulls the body back, giving the dancer or fighter a solid, earthed platform from which to move forwards again.

The Saiidi stick dance is also known as the 'Dance of the Arab Stallions', because it is believed that the rhythm and masculine steps and postures emulate the strong, gallant moves of that much-respected male Arabian horse. It is splendid to witness the horses themselves 'dancing' to the rhythm. On a balmy evening outside the Cairo Marriott, I saw a majestic display that had been organised as part of a lavish wedding celebration. The bride was seated in an extravagant carriage, pulled along by six white stallions moving in time with the drummers leading the entourage.

Egypt's southerners, the Saiidis, brought much of the basic foot, hip and drum work to the style that later became an intrinsic component of every folkloric show. Mahmoud Reda, himself a magnificent dancer who performed Saiidi-style in many movies, introduced the

Salah to cinema with his dynamic troupe choreographies. One will often see similar choreographies by a troupe of male dancers clad in simple turban-style headscarves and long, brown galebeyas. The dance is very powerful when performed by an all-male ensemble, although the mock fighting element found its way onto stage as entertainment through the play between a female dancer and the two warriors 'fighting' over her.

When performing with men in Saiidi dances, as part of the group, women normally dance without the staffs. Their hip work and turns, though, interpret the heavy rhythm. However, when performing as a solo or lead role, the female dancer will usually wear her galebeya, headdress and heavy gold jewellery as she wields a lightweight cane. Nagua Fouad demonstrates the cane dance as the lead dancer in her video, 'Layali Nagua Fouad'. These days, the female baladi dancer will often use the cane as a prop that represents the male persona in Egyptian dance. It has recently been taken into the realm of cabaret, though most Egyptian dancers will wear a baladi dress or a more traditional outfit when performing this style of dance.

KYLE ELLIS PERFORMING
THE STICK DANCE

21

EGYPTIAN BALADI

The rhythm of the tabla is the heartbeat of Egypt. It is a steady earthy pulse that sets the pace of life—weighty, grounded, sensual. The dance of Egypt is baladi, meaning literally 'of the country'. This deep-seated dance style is more closely related to folk than to classical forms of Middle Eastern dance, yet it has been wrought to a fine art.

Baladi is an improvised cultural dance performed by a soloist. The dancer interprets the music through controlled body movements, mainly with swerving hip moves such as undulations, figure-eights, drops and shimmies, but also with gesture. The nature of baladi is its steady flow of energy from reserved to exuberant, typified in the progression of many of the musical compositions that baladi dancers follow in Egypt, either at family parties or on stage. The famous performers of the early Egyptian cinema industry made baladi popular, adding a touch of city-girl glamour by way of costume.

Traditional baladi dancers incorporate headgear as an important part of their costume—a veil, scarf or headpiece of coins, passed down from earlier generations in Islamic society. This aspect of the costume matches the quieter side of the dance. It is, after all, essentially a modest dance, feminine and contained. At the same time it possesses great power in its robustness and dynamic confidence. Baladi costume is normally a body-fitting kaftan with hip scarf and headscarf. It was only with the growth of Egyptian cinema and cabaret shows that modern baladi dancers began wearing the two-piece costume. Some believe baladi should not cross these boundaries, while others are inspired by the interpretive quality of the dance—which is more important to them than strict stylistic codes. The underlying control in this mostly exuberant style of bellydance reflects the people's sentiments in a subtle way.

A city dance that had its roots in the country villages—the 'real home' of the people—baladi emerged as an aspect of urban folklore. As Egypt became industrialised, many of the farmers and villagers were forced by economic crisis to move to the large city. In Cairo, the expanding population meant that there was often no work. Among the ghettos that consequently formed, music and dance became an outlet for the sense of frustration over living in a crowded urban environment far from home. Songs about yearning and missing one's love or home served as symbols of displacement. The country or baladi people expressed themselves in song or dance that made constant reference to heartfelt longing. With this music they could recall happier times, the gaiety and simplicity of traditional life. In spite of the sadness of this nostalgia, the rhythm of baladi and the corresponding style of dance are in themselves celebratory. It is a dance performed for joy. People will often break into a few notes or gestures of baladi song or dance as a spontaneous response to a humorous situation. In fact, baladi creates its own sense of fun.

It is not difficult to see, then, how baladi is more than a musical movement or a style of dance. It is the very essence and rhythm of Egyptian life, internalised in the people's movements, their walk, their manner. The grandiose gestures often seen in Western versions of bellydancing appear overstated in comparison with the ease and naturalness of the Egyptian girls' dancing. The movements in Egyptian baladi are all the more felt for their subtlety. There is an emotive drive which intensifies the dance, a way of moving to more than just rhythm. Whilst the women of Cairo are seemingly born with an innate sense of rhythm and ability to interpret musical nuance, it is the way they feel the ballads, transmitting anew the sentiments of the people already articulated in music, that transcends the mere physical act of dancing. And they do this through the tilt of the head, the expression of the face and the delicate gestures of the hands and eyes.

Baladi dance incorporates the use of baladi personas. It is a means of expressing both the feminine and masculine genders in the songs. Often, as the dancer mimes a story, she changes character and movement accordingly. The Saiidi ballads speak of an El Saiid warrior, and the dancer represents the male stick dancer with her cane and heavier hip movements. She may also take on the role of the head village woman, the malemma, with a smooth and grounded assertiveness, sometimes using the prop of a pot or basket on the head—or even just the gesture of it—to bring this character to life. Whether mimicking the shy maiden or the mother-in-law, the baladi dancer metamorphoses from one traditional character to another. On stage, this immersion in the theatrical element of baladi is what enriches the dancer's art.

One of the most spectacular baladi props is the shamadan or candelabra. The dancer wears the heavy brass head piece with up to two dozen lit candles as she performs shimmies and torso undulations. The flickering flames are believed to ward off evil spirits and the 'evil eye', hence the shamadan is a popular baladi tradition at weddings and festivals.

Badia Masabni, a famous baladi dancer in the 1920s went on to leave a legacy of dancers trained by her, namely Tahiya Karioka and Samia Gamal. Tahiya Karioka, Nagua

THE SHAMADAN CANDELABRA DANCE IS A TRADITIONAL EGYPTIAN FOLK STYLE OF DANCING WHERE THE DANCER WEARS A HEAVY BRASS CANDELABRA ON HER HEAD. IT IS HEAVY AND THE LIT CANDLES ARE SENSITIVE TO SUDDEN MOVEMENTS, SO THE DANCER USES EARTHY SLOW BALADI MOVES TO STAY CENTRED

Fouad, Fifi Abduo and—nowadays—Lucy are baladi dancers who became famous as 'oriental dancers'. Tahiya, in the many films of the early Egyptian cinema industry, performed in traditional assyuti-style costume, a long dress made from a sheer cotton mesh, emblazoned with pressed silver. Tahiya, the daughter of a Muslim sheikh, was punished severely by her brothers for her active love of dance in her youth. They would beat her to discourage her from becoming a dancer. However, she ran away from home and eventually went on to become one of the most famous and respected Egyptian dancers and cinema actresses of all time. Her story is, in a sense, encapsulated in the baladi style, with its many apparent contradictions.

One of Cairo's most popular dancers today is Lucy. Celebrated for her elegant, demure style reminiscent of Tahiya Karioka, her body acknowledges every small beat of the drum and melodic nuance. Although she is one of the most renowned baladi dancers of our own times, Lucy incorporates other cultural dance styles into her routine, like flamenco and North African. She has a way of working these into the more traditional dance styles of Cairo so that they mesh well. 'Dancing is my art,' says Lucy. 'It is my femininity, my beauty, my strength.'

STREET WEDDING ON A BRIDGE OVER THE NILE

22

ALEXANDRIAN MILAYA DANCE

The milaya il'laff is a type of oriental shawl which gained popularity in Egypt in the 1930s and 1940s. It alluringly conceals and reveals, being made of a dark and heavy fabric that can nonetheless be wrapped tightly around the body. In Egypt's main urban centres of Alexandria and Cairo, this shawl made a cosmopolitan statement. From its humble origins as village dress, inspired by the shawls the Alexandrian Greek men wore, the milaya soon became a popular Egyptian fashion item for women, around the 1950s. It was often accompanied by a knitted face veil called a 'bourka' and worn around a tight-fitting dress with a ruffled neckline and hem.

At family parties and local celebrations, often held outdoors by the sea, the women would slowly begin dancing with the milaya, using the re-wrapping gesture as part of their dance. The tightly wrapped shawl would accentuate the movements of the hips and waist, and this, coupled with the throwing of the milaya over the arms, became the basis for a stylised Alexandrian 'fishing' dance. Before the men went out to sea, the women would dance playfully on the pier, clicking together the heels of their sheb-sheb (clogs) and walking with a teasing sway of their hips to 'reel in the fishermen' with mock gestures.

Egyptian village women continued this tradition, embellishing the dances of their family gatherings with a simple shoulder or hip scarf. In fact, since earliest times, the scarf or veil has been an integral part of oriental dance. But the 'dance of the milaya', in particular, came to represent the dual, subtle yet flirtatious aspect of Middle Eastern dance and is an integral part of Egyptian baladi.

The Egyptian milaya is very heavy and is usually folded in half during the dance. It reflects a style of baladi and the music is normally an up-tempo, highly spirited Egyptian song with colloquial lyrics. The hip moves are also heavy, yet playful and bouncy, often a humorous parody of a saucy, gum-chewing 'street girl'. Fifi Abdou often does the 'Eskendereya' or milaya dance of Alexandria. She once danced for four hours in a play called Eshta we Assel ('Cream and Honey'), changing costume and dance style thirteen times! Mahmoud Reda and Farida Fahmy have choreographed some stunning milaya troupe work, which has featured in Egyptian films and theatre.

The milaya dance is a popular item of traditional Middle Eastern dance repertoire, possibly because it speaks of an enjoyable era in recent Egyptian history, when the economy was improving and women experienced a freedom and flirtatiousness that came with a new, fashionable veil.

LYNNELL WITH EGYPTIAN MILAYA

23
LEBANON

Lebanon has a long history of dance going back to the Phoenician period from 2500 BC to 400 BC. During this era, the Phoenicians worshipped the fertility goddess Astarte, whose cult involved a fertility dance similar to bellydancing. As far inland as Damascus and in many cities on the Mediterranean coast that became part of the Assyrian empire in 743 BC, masterful artefacts—including statuettes of female dancers—were created by Phoenician carvers and stonemasons. Today, still, from sprightly group folk dances like the dabke to the solo bellydance, the dance arts of Lebanon are celebratory.

Modern Lebanese bellydance, often attributed to the legacy of the late Nadia Gamal, of Greek–Italian parentage, highlights the popularity of the raqs sharqi style in Lebanon. In the earlier part of this century, many Lebanese stars like Naima Akef, and famous oud player, singer and actor Farid El Attrache (who was also a Druze prince), followed the bright lights of the booming Egyptian cinema industry and found fame. However, these days the cosmopolitan lifestyle of Beirut—known as the 'Riviera of the Middle East'—boasts a glamorous media industry and elite socialite scene. Lebanese bellydancers seem to have retained the classicism of oriental dance with a feisty, modern edge. The style is highly interpretive, yet more energetic and directed at entertainment than Egyptian dance. Recently, costumes have become wildly experimental, with everything from feathers to hotpants making a debut. The extravagant fashion sense of the Lebanese may well be driven by their French connection. It has a very European flair compared with much of the Middle East, with the possible exception of western Turkey.

AMERA REGULARLY PERFORMED IN LEBANON

In Lebanon, bellydancers appear on television and entertain the social set on ornate ferries drifting on Beirut waters on summer nights. Popular, attractive dancers become national icons. Dancers like Hwaida Hazchem and Neriman Aboud have audiences waiting with baited breath, eager to see which costume and risqué new moves will be aired on the next LBC special! With such media hype, often more attention revolves around the presentation of the dancer than her ability. Still, there are many dedicated dancers who continually work at raising the profile of Lebanese dance as an art. Amani is an especially popular artist who has lifted the standards of oriental dance in Lebanon with a sincere interpretation of oriental music. Although a busy performance and teaching schedule takes her around the world, she shares her love of oriental dance with many students and teachers.

But Western countries such as Australia have their share of great dancers of Lebanese origin too. Melbourne's talented dancer and teacher, Claire Naffah, represents all that is best in Lebanese raqs sharqi. Her understanding of music and gesture, coupled with the training she received from the late Nadia Gamal, has made her one of the most sought after dancers for Middle Eastern cultural events in Australia. Sydney dancer Amera Eid, also inspired by the Lebanese style, regularly travels to Beirut to perform in the city's top restaurants and clubs.

EVA CASS, POPULAR GREEK BELLYDANCER

24

GREEK CHIFTETELLI

Greek bellydancing is a high-spirited, sensual celebration of the body dating back three thousand years to Helladic Greece and Minoan Crete. The Greek chiftetelli is most similar to Turkish bellydance, with its many shimmies, pelvic tilts and hip lifts. Its origins are the same as Turkish dance, stemming from temple dancing thousands of years ago when the Greeks worshipped several goddesses—including Artemis, Aphrodite and Gaia. Associated with love, beauty and music, these early religious cults of Grecian influence celebrated feminine fertility through dance. Dancers of the Temple of Aphrodite would perform in exchange for money, which in turn, went towards maintenance of the temple.

During the Classical Greek period, symmetry and sensuality featured prominently in sculpture and painting. The Greeks believed art was a means of replicating the perfect images of their gods and heroes—beautifully sculpted bodies dancing and posing. The aesthetically inclined civilisation also invented a style of dance that featured movements like 'gliding', 'turning with a skip' and 'stomping on grapes'! The movements had a similar quality to bellydance, with more refined and classical arm gesture. Classical Greek dance was a popular sports and dance subject earlier this century, taught at many schools throughout Europe. Babylon, cradle of oriental dance, was once the capital city of the vast Hellenised parts of the Near East during the reign of Alexander the Great. The Egyptian city of Alexandria, founded by him, still carries the legacies of cultural merging. The Alexandrian milaya shawl, a popular bellydance accessory, was originally a garment worn by Greek men. A Hellenistic bronze statue of a veiled dancer dated at approximately 225 BC, believed to be from Alexandria, seems to sway her hips to a slow rhythm, wrapping her shawl around her hips. The gesture looks similar to the way a milaya is used in dance.

Sensual, mesmerising instrumentals and feisty celebration dances have evolved over the centuries using the bazouki, the Greek version of the lute. The Greeks have a name for bellydancing that translates as 'the mortar and pestle dance'—suggesting a grinding action of the hips. More recent bellydance styles emanating from that part of the world have followed the Turkish manner of dance—fast and titillating. The modern bellydance is normally a nightclub feature show, the dancer(s) appearing in glittering cabaret costume. Greek bellydance also includes folk movements like cross-stepping in a grapevine fashion, hopping from one leg to the other and shoulder shimmying with the arms open. And, sometimes . . . breaking plates!

25

TURKISH BELLYDANCE

Cabaret bellydance

In the seaside city of Marmaris, I visited an old castle that had been converted into a nightclub. Three spangled dancers appeared in a thick haze of green-coloured smoke, their feathered headdresses visible above the cloud. To the pulse of techno music they began thrusting, bumping and turning in perfect cabaret unison, reminiscent of Las Vegas showgirls. Slender, sculpted bodies clad in strategically placed triangles of green sequins writhed as the music continued its pulsating beat. For me, the most fascinating item of their costume was the sheer face veil worn by each. They did not once remove this piece of armour, but maintained their air of mystery despite their being so very nearly naked. This is the domain of tourists, nightlife and the seedier side of town.

Capital cities in the Middle East, seething with tourists and Western concepts of entertainment, tend to breed such styles of dance. I had already witnessed this phenomenon in Cairo, but more so in the heavily European-influenced city of Istanbul where the influx of Western tourists is accountable for the gimmicky nature of the dance. Bellydancers are constantly appearing in skimpy costumes to sell tabloids, CDs and postcards, and frequently wriggle their hips on Turkish MTV music clips.

The Turkish bellydancer is called a rakkassa, meaning 'dancer'. Turkish dance movements are higher, lighter and faster than the deep-seated baladi styles from Egypt. The predominant move is the hip lift or tilt that corresponds to the more frequent taks played on the Turkish dumbek. The drumbeat can be very fast and repetitive, driving a constant hip and foot synchronicity with the music. Zills are played to the faster rhythms. Rakass is a dynamic, overt cabaret style of dancing where the dancer's rapid hip movements serve to excite the audience. Shimmies, pelvic gyrations and abdominal muscle manipulations often accompany floor work.

The chiftetelli, a specialised style of dance and music popular in both Turkey and Greece, originating in pre-Turkish civilisation, evolved over the centuries as a sensual bellydance—a fertility dance. Much later, the Ottoman harems were home to seductive dance as entertainment art. Theirs was the era of opulence and grandeur, richness and sensual indulgence. In the late 1800s the French gave the name of *danse du ventre* or 'dance of the belly' to this tantalising women's dance from Turkey. Until recently, classical Turkish dancers like the real-life princess, Princess Banu, had lifted the dance to the realm of elite artistic expression. During the past century, however, whether it is performed for tourists or enthusiastic locals, Turkish dance has tended increasingly towards the burlesque.

It is a known fact that Turkish women love to dance, and most are exceptional dancers. The people enjoy their music. Even beyond folk dancing styles, they celebrate with up-tempo chiftetelli and modern songs with traditional rhythms. However, bellydancing has developed a questionable reputation. If this harsh judgment stems in part from the Turks' own recognition of the way the dance appears to have degenerated, it is also grounded in a general belief that the first bellydancers in their country were foreigners. Centuries ago, Jews and gypsies danced in the streets for money as they travelled through the towns. The gypsies in particular became enmeshed over time with prostitution and 'selling the dance' for a living. Still, the bellydance of Turkey thrives in its own country and continues to fascinate tourists.

Folk dance—Karsilama

The Turkish Karsilama survives as a folk dance with a rhythm played in traditional 9/8 time. The dance is also known as the 'mastika', literally meaning 'drinking song', with a repetitive pattern of three walking steps followed by three faster bounces, twists or hip tilts. The dance, performed by men and women, consists of a sprightly step on the right foot, left foot and then feet together, followed by a bounce on the toes with a quick bow of the head. The latter part can be exchanged for little pelvic tilts or twists. Sometimes the feet cross over, with a double step to change feet on the fast accents. The dancer pushes the hips forwards and the arms back. The sequences are often repeated four times, in a square format, i.e. facing the front, side, back and side.

26

TRIBAL, GYPSY AND TRANCE DANCES

The dances of the North African and Middle Eastern deserts have inspired some distinctive styles of dance, including tribal, gypsy and trance dancing. The movements, rhythms and costumes related to tribal dance have been adapted from many disparate groups within the Middle East: the nomadic Bedouins, the Moroccan Amazigh (widely known as Berbers), the Ouled Nail dancers of the Northern Sahara—cultures where folklore meets tribal life. With all these styles, the rhythms are repetitive, earthy and trance-like, supporting group participation. The movements are also very grounded, as the predominant instruments belong to the family of drums.

Ghawazee

The Ghawazee dancers of Egypt were a nomadic gypsy tribe who eventually settled there, despite discrimination from the Egyptian villagers. The lively dance of the Ghawazee later became a primary source of inspiration for indigenous Egyptian dance. Their style consists of simple, repetitive hip lifts, turns and constant playing of finger cymbals. Like most Middle Eastern tribal and trance styles of dance, the Ghawazee rhythms progressively get faster with the finale building to a frenzied and ecstatic shaking of the hips.

Trance dances

Trance dancing, like the Egyptian zaar and the religious ceremonies of the Tuareg tribe, involve rhythmic shaking of the head and upper body until the dancer enters a trance-like

AMANDA IN GHAWAZEE COSTUME

state, where the movement is totally free-form. The dance serves as a ritual 'exorcism' where the 'djinn' or evil spirits are believed to be driven from the body by the drums and the energetic body vibrations. The dancing may go on for hours, gradually building speed until the dancer pushes the body to the point of collapse or total physical exhaustion.

Tribal

The primary characteristics of tribal dance are strength and kinship—dancing and celebrating within the tribe or group. Far from the solo dance-art, which is for show, the tribal bellydance involves a group improvising together, each falling into sync with the others' movements. In tribal bellydance the rhythmic patterns of the music prompt hip lifts, simple steps and earthy, grounded shimmy walks. The lower body does most of the movement, while the upper body remains fairly poised and stationary.

American troupe 'Fat Chance Bellydance' recently revived the tribal style adding its own contemporary influences.

EGYPTIAN ZAAR MOVEMENTS

27

OTHER MIDDLE EASTERN DANCE STYLES

Persian

Persian dance music is lighter than other styles of bellydance. The arms, hands, head and eyes play a more important role in this ancient art. Footwork, like the small hopping step with a continuous travelling flow, is kept light and nimble. The arm positions highlight the head slides, rib cage lifts and hip moves, many of which are performed on the horizontal plane. Persian costume consists of a vest worn over loose cotton blouses or dresses, with an intricate design embroidered with gold thread. The veil and small hand scarves feature prominently.

There is also a lot of gesture and mime; a particular favourite of mine is the 'Grooming Dance'. The dancer, clothed in flowing white cotton garments, mimes the delicate preparation of a young lady awaiting her suitor. She applies her kohl and adorns herself with her finest robes, perfumes and jewellery. She pretends to sip wine from an imaginary goblet, dancing more merrily with every swig. Looking repeatedly at her clock, noticing that her suitor is late, she continues drinking and dancing with an increasing number of twirls and shimmies. When she finally greets her suitor at the door, she falls drunkenly into his arms!

Khaleegee

The khaleegee from the Arabian Gulf is a gliding, small-stepping dance performed to the khaleegee rhythm, with the dancer in a long, wide, embroidered veil-dress. The dress looks like two long veils that have been sewn together. The dancer lifts the veil-dress lightly, dancing with it held out in the front. The dress fabric serves as a prop to embellish the dance. Sometimes the hair is flicked from side to side, and the overall quality of the dance is a graceful, trance-like gliding.

Andalusian

Andalusian dance from Morocco is a North African–Spanish hybrid, evoking images of the palaces of Granada. It has the feel of flamenco dance, combined with the lightness and ease of bellydance. The Reda Academy in Egypt often incorporates the Andalusian dance into its cultural repertoire. The costume is usually pantaloons and vest, and it is often danced with flowing veils attached to the headpiece and covering the dancer's back. Much of both Moroccan and Andalusian dance consists of crescent-moon movements, where arms alternate in balletic poses—one arm raised above the head and the other resting in front of the belly, palm facing upwards. The body also stretches with the upstretched arm, creating a gentle curve like a crescent moon.

Amazigh and Tuareg

In an area of North Africa represented mostly by the country of Morocco, two village peoples who regularly celebrate with dance are the Amazigh (Berbers) of the Atlas Mountains and the Tuareg tribe. The Amazigh reveal a Spanish influence in their dance style—heavy and grounded, with stepping movements that drive the foot into the ground and the hip upwards. The Tuareg, also known as the 'blue people' because they use indigo to paint and protect their faces from the sun, have developed a ceremonial trance dance. Traditional Tuareg costuming consists of a simple blue cotton dress, with tribal metal necklaces and special ceremonial beads woven into African-style braided hair. Each bead signifies a special event. This dance involves a flicking motion of the hands away from the body, and in this respect it resembles the Egyptian zaar. However, whereas the zaar uses much head flicking to induce trance and metaphorically 'shake the djinn (or evil spirits) out of the body', the head is far less involved in the Tuareg dance, which focuses on the flicking motion to release accumulated energies.

'DANCING WITH A GROUP OF
WOMEN CONNECTS US IN A SPIRIT OF FUN;
WE LAUGH A LOT,
WE FEEL YOUNG AGAIN!'

AYESHA, ADANI KHALEEGEE

DANCERS

$\mathscr{P}$ART FIVE

COSTUME AND PERFORMANCE

28

FOLKLORIC COSTUME

Throughout the Middle East, folkloric costume is the traditional attire for provincial dances. It tells where the people and the dance come from. In Egypt, for example, the simple cotton galebeyas that Nubian dancers wear contrast starkly with the colourful dresses of the women of the Fayoum Oasis. The long black plaits, the headscarves and billowing dresses of the fellaha (farm girl) are very different from the slim-fitting, silver-embossed Assyut kaftan, from the town of the same name. The Andalusian dancers of Morocco wear floating layers of skirts, blouses and pantaloons, while the Amazigh sport dresses and long, full skirts in colourful tribal weaves. Even in Turkish and Persian dance, the folkloric costume is a modest creation of pantaloons and long, slim dresses. In the Gulf region, a beautifully embroidered, wide dress accentuates the moves of the khaleegee dance style. Two things that seem to be standard in the arena of folkloric costume, though, are the long galebeya and the headscarf.

A basic folkloric costume has a kaftan or galebeya, a headscarf, a hip scarf and skirts or pantaloons. There are often many layers and the colours are usually rich and earthy. Add to this a smattering of coins and antique jewellery, and the look is not only beautiful, but also highly authentic to Middle Eastern dance. Many women find this style of costume more flattering than the two-piece cabaret costume. In fact, the way the dress hugs the curves of the body, with the scarf emphasis at the hips, is beguiling.

The folkloric apparel suits movements and rhythms that are strong and grounded. It is good for dancing with the stick and for baladi. If you find the folkloric style of dress appealing, follow this basic guide to sewing your own galebeya:

- Choose fabric that looks rich and exotic—deep colours are often the most flattering. A stretch knit will be easier to wear, but a quality cotton weave will look traditional.
- Sew the fabric into a simple long dress, attaching sleeves that flare out towards the edges.
- Slits in the sides will make movement easier.
- Decorate the neckline, sleeves or hem, including all around the edges of the slits, with coins.

The scarves can also be cut from this fabric and coins sewn along the edges. Wear one on the head and the other around the hips. Traditional, heavy jewellery looks best with this kind of costume—big coin earrings and neckpieces.

The tribal costume is more colourful and layered than the folkloric costume. The layers of skirts, inspired by the Ghawazee dancers of the Egyptian desert, are usually made from a heavy cotton fabric. The scarves and belts are thicker and heavier, borrowing from the hardy designs of the nomads—thick tassels, camel hair tapestries and rope. The top part of the costume consists of vests and blouses, with heavy coin decoration. Presentation is completed with layered headwear or coin-covered face veils, tattoos, heavy copper jewellery and finger cymbals.

A VEIL COVERING THE HAIR, HELD IN PLACE WITH A SMALLER SCARF WRAPPED AROUND THE FOREHEAD. THIS MAY BE DECORATED WITH COINS

HEAVY COIN NECKLACE OR THE TRADITIONAL CRESCENT MOON NECKPIECE FOR BALADI

ENSURE THERE IS ENOUGH ROOM TO LIFT YOUR ARMS OR LEAVE A SLIT UNDER THE ARM

WIDE SLEEVES, SOMETIMES SHEER

SASH WORN LOW ON HIPS

A NARROW-FITTING DRESS CAN BE MADE WITH STRETCH FABRIC, EGYPTIAN ASSYUTI (SEE PAGE 115)

A MODEST SPLIT FOR EASE OF MOVEMENT

29

ASSYUTI

How many European women, I wonder, would have received in the 1930s or 1940s a parcel of fabric as a gift from a man at war, and upon unfolding the tissue paper, found a long piece of soft black cotton material woven like fine lace and enmeshed with a pattern of hundreds of pieces of beaten silver? A friend tells me her father brought just such a piece of fabric back for her mother in the 1940s. For years after their parents died she and her sister shared this legacy, each wearing it only on special occasions, neither remembering exactly what it was or where it was from. Now she knows it even has a name all to itself.

In the early Egyptian cinema industry of the 1930s and 1940s, when dance featured prominently in many of the old classical films, the dancer would often perform in a long black dress emblazoned with delicate pieces of silver. Like the milaya il'laff, the baladi dresses of that era made a very cosmopolitan fashion statement. They originated in a simple town on the Nile called Assyut, which became popular for its production of a fine cotton net fabric with small plaques of silver worked into patterns throughout. It is recognised that this stunning fabric inspired the opulent European evening gowns of the 1920s. Since the eighteenth century, when Europeans began emulating the lavish decoration from the 'exotic East', this fabric was brought back to the finest dressmakers on the continent. At the turn of the century, Queen Charlotte had her wedding dress designed with a layer of assyuti-style fabric.

Assyuti costuming is normally associated with Egyptian baladi—the urban folk form of dance done by women. Its pieces of flashing silver seem to flow on the body, highlighting the grounded, stylised movements focused around hip, shoulder and belly. Usually worn with a simple coin scarf around the hips, and matching decorated headscarf, the assyuti is an elegant, stately dress that speaks of glamour and ethnicity.

Famous baladi dancers of Egypt, like Tahiya Karioka, Nagua Fouad and Fifi Abdou, often performed traditional Egyptian folkloric dances in assyuti costume, sometimes in red fabric, although black is more traditional. Accompanying this style of dance are the sagat (finger cymbals), the cane (as in the Saiidi style of dance) and sometimes even a clay pot or tambourine. A necessary item of dance costume in Egypt in the 1950s, the assyuti dress is becoming increasingly popular with Western dancers exploring traditional Egyptian dance. It is chosen for its simple line, allowing the body freedom of movement, and its glittering antique appeal.

HENNA, KOHL AND HEADWEAR

Henna is used by Middle Eastern women for both beauty and protection. For thousands of years, henna has been known to have healing and medicinal qualities. In Islamic religious practice, its application is synonymous with luck and spiritual cleansing. Egyptians and Turks believe henna removes the 'evil eye', while in Morocco, pregnant women get their ankles decorated at seven months for a 'safe pregnancy'. They even plaster the baby's navel when it is born, as henna contains cleansing and soothing qualities. In the desert, henna is applied to the foreheads of children with fever, as it cools the body.

Many cultures, including Moroccan, Algerian, Egyptian, Sudanese and Turkish, use henna to decorate women's hands and feet for weddings and ceremonies. Dance and henna are closely linked in folkloric tradition, because henna is often used in ceremonial 'rites of passage'—when a girl enters puberty or gets married, for example. The crushed leaves of the plant are mixed with special oils and pure water to make a thick paste, which is used to create decorative tattoos on the hands, feet, ankles or belly. It is then fixed with a sugar and lemon glaze, and repeatedly moistened so the colour turns a deep red-brown over the course of approximately twelve hours. Sometimes the hair, fingertips or soles of the feet are stained with henna. Natural henna is always red or brown, and lasts for up to three weeks. 'Black henna', popular in Sudan, contains petroleum which can damage the skin.

The blue pigment used for permanent tattooing of the chin and forehead in Moroccan, Turkish and Egyptian villages is indigo pigment. The symbolic tattoos were usually marriage and tribal markings that indicated which family the woman belonged to. A popular make-up trick for the tribal or assyuti dance styles is to draw on these delicate chin tattoos with navy blue eyeliner.

Kohl

The mysterious dark eyes of the East often appear so to Westerners because of the way they are heavily rimmed with kohl. The Persians even have a dance mimicking the application of kohl. Like henna, kohl is believed to be a sacred powder that has protective qualities, and is not prohibited in Islam. On the contrary, it is seen as a sign of beauty and holy adornment. Traditionally, kohl was worn on the inner eyelids for healing and protection for the eyes against the dusty, dry environment.

For bellydance performance, before applying either the powdered or crayon kohl, make sure the eye area is clean and a foundation base has been applied. This prevents smearing and makes the kohl glide on more easily. Draw a long line above the upper eyelashes, thicker towards the outer edges, creating the illusion of long, almond-shaped eyes. Trace a line under the bottom eyelashes and soften the look with a smudging stick. Then apply a layer of gold dust or shimmering eye shadow to the eyelid. Finish with mascara. Remember, when performing, use enough make-up to accentuate your features; a fancy costume can be overpowering on a pale face!

Headwear

Headwear always completes the folkloric or tribal costume. From metres of rich fabric, woven into turbans and fixed with coins and antique jewellery, to simple headscarves, head accessories always add a touch of the exotic. A simple way of fixing a headscarf to the hair is with clips or a headband. To create a turban, first put up the hair in a bun and cover with a cotton scarf. Then begin wrapping metres of fabric around the head, until the effect is quite bulky. When the turban is fixed in place with pins, decorate it with twisted ribbons of rope or fabric, coins and pendants. You can get very inventive. Add dangling coin earrings to the centre and sides for a truly exotic effect.

To complement your folkloric, gypsy or tribal costume, other accessories to look out for are thick brass bangles, anklets, coin necklaces, armbands and coin belts. These can often be found at Indian suppliers, markets and second-hand stores.

31

CABARET COSTUME

The glitzy cabaret costume appeals to both the East and West. It is usually comprised of a decorated bra and a matching decorated belt that is worn over a skirt. But it would not be complete without the accessories—and then some! Beaded fringing made from glass beads, coins, sequins and rhinestones, that capture light and movement, create the bespangled look of the cabaret costume. Too much is still not enough! And the fun part of all this is being inventive!

The bra

Find a firm cupped bra that is a size larger than you normally wear. The extra room seems to diminish with heavy covering and decoration. You can either cut away the cups and cover them individually, then sew on a back and neck strap, or you can cover the entire bra—which is trickier. Cover the bra in the fabric of your choice in a base colour, whether it be gold, black or coloured fabric. Material like lycra or sequin-stretch fabric covers well. Many costume makers suggest avoiding covering the straps of the bra as they are; it looks more flattering to sew an entirely new strap—usually a thicker one. Decide whether you want the bra to do up with hook and eyes from the back or front, then fit it to the bust before decorating.

To decorate the bra, draw up a design and begin to sew on sequins, rhinestones, coins or other motifs. The best way to sew on beaded fringing is either to buy the fringing (usually made in Egypt) and sew on the ribbon it is attached to or take a ribbon and bead your own fringe. If you are beading fringe with glass seed beads and bugle beads, use strong thread and a good backstitch for safety. Then attach the ribbon to the bra, covering any overlap with the same fabric as used before.

The belt

Design your belt from tracing paper first to make sure it fits comfortably. It should sit well below the navel, low on the hips. A dip in the middle is very flattering, as it follows the female shape better. Decide where you wish the belt to do up, taking into account that a skirt will be worn underneath. Once you have a design template, cut the same shape from a stiffened Vilene or other strong facing fabric. Then cover it in the same fabric as the bra and decorate to match. If you are making fringe, design its shape, then sew it onto a ribbon, which you later apply.

The skirt

A full circle skirt normally takes 6 metres of fabric. Choose fabric that falls well, like satin or other materials used for ball gowns. Lay out the fabric on the floor, at its full length, then fold in four parts. Measure your hip to toe, allowing for hemming, and draw the marks on a broomstick. Then, with the help of a friend, use the broomstick as a yard measure to outline a perfect quarter circle. Once cut, you should have two quarter circles and a full half circle. Sew the parts together and hem, then insert elastic at the top. The circle skirt should sit just on the hips and be covered by the belt.

A straight skirt is simpler. Just cut a front and back panel, and sew together. Or for an overlay skirt made of chiffon, that sits over the circle skirt, attach two separate panels to elastic and hem all round.

Accessories

Head, wrist and ankle bands can be made from a Vilene base and then covered and decorated in the same fabric as the bra and belt. Fringe can also be added for movement. Beaded earrings and necklaces are also attractive accessories for a cabaret costume.

CREATE NEW STRAPS FOR THE BRA.
A HALTERNECK IS SAFER WHEN PERFORMING,
AS THERE IS NO CHANCE OF THE STRAP
SLIPPING OFF THE SHOULDER.

USE A FITTED BRA WITH CUPS MADE
FROM A FIRM, THICK FABRIC THAT
WILL KEEP ITS SHAPE WHEN COVERED. PUSH-UP
BRAS ARE OFTEN THE MOST FLATTERING.

ACCESSORIES ACCENTUATE HAND
MOVEMENTS AND COMPLETE
THE COSTUME.

FRINGING ON THE BRA SHOULD SUIT THE
TORSO. SHORT FRINGING ELONGATES A SHORT
TORSO, AND LONG FRINGING LOOKS
BETTER ON A LONG TORSO.

THE BELT BASE SHOULD BE CUT FROM A
HEAVY FABRIC, COVERED, AND
THEN DECORATED WITH SEQUINS,
COINS OR BEADS. FRINGING
MADE FROM GLASS BEADS
ENHANCES MOVEMENT.

SKIRTS CAN BE SIMPLE AND STRAIGHT OR
FULL CIRCLE AND MULTI-LAYERED. WHEN
LAYERING FABRICS, ALWAYS USE DENSE
FABRIC UNDERNEATH AND WEAR THE
SILK OR CHIFFON LAYERS OVER THE TOP.
TUCKING SKIRT EDGES IN AT THE HIP
CREATES AN ATTRACTIVE RUFFLE AND
ACCENTUATES THE DANCER'S HIP MOVEMENTS.

32

PERFORMANCE

Not everyone goes into bellydancing to become a performer of the art. Many people are happy to use it as a recreational pastime, purely for fun and relaxation. But sometimes there comes with these exciting new skills a desire to show them off—perhaps at a 'hafla' (Arabic for 'festive gathering') or a students' bellydance party or for a group of friends or family. Here are some hints for making the performance a success:

- Know your music well and practise in front of a friend or teacher for feedback.
- Put your music onto a quality tape, with a short entry and exit piece added if necessary.
- Keep it short and dynamic!
- Practise in your costume so you feel comfortable in it.
- Arrange to be introduced—write it on paper if you don't know the person doing the introduction.
- When performing, smile, breathe and do your best!

When the dancer becomes more skilled, there is often plenty of opportunity to perform. Festivals, displays and other public events are forums where performers can show their skills. However, it does take time and patience to become a professional performer/entertainer—usually not before several years of committed dancing, so make sure you are really ready for a paid job in a restaurant or at a party. Here are some helpful tips for dancing for larger audiences:

- Know your audience and any appropriate cultural customs, for example, certain music and rhythms are appropriate for an Egyptian wedding—like the traditional zaffa; whilst a Turkish or Persian party usually requires the correct music. When dancing for a Middle Eastern audience, especially, it is paramount to know that your music is what their dancers usually perform to.
- Prepare your costume, music, spare pins, zills and make-up, and pack neatly in a case or bag.
- Make sure you know your music thoroughly and that it has been recorded well, with good levels, neat joins and an entry and exit piece.
- If you are wearing your costume on arrival, make sure it is covered up and avoid showing the costume before or after performance. Only during!
- Be punctual, leaving plenty of time for parking and costume changes.
- Tell the announcer how you would like to be announced and give clear instructions for music cues.
- When performing, act confident, strong and beautiful, showing the best of your art.
- Should you accept tips from the audience? That is a personal decision. To avoid people getting too close for comfort, it is up to you not to get too close to the audience. However, remember that tipping is a custom in many Middle Eastern countries, so accepting a tip may be appropriate.
- Sometimes people will want to get up to dance with you or you may select an audience member to join your performance. This usually guarantees much laughter and merriment. If so, stay in control and give them a polite 'thanks' when you need them to sit down.
- Discuss your fee and method of payment beforehand, and refuse to be bargained down. Stand your ground when it comes to your worth as a performer—top dancers are always in demand—and be well aware of the current acceptable 'market rate'.

• Before, during and after the show, maintain professionalism. Be polite, courteous and helpful.

Dancing for others can be the greatest pleasure for a bellydancer. Just remember to practise performing for friends and fellow bellydancers when the opportunity arises, because practice makes perfect!

'FOR ME, PERFORMING FOR AN AUDIENCE IS A CHANCE TO BE CREATIVE AND PASSIONATE. I ESPECIALLY LOVE THE CABARET STYLE, WHERE I CAN BE AS DRAMATIC AND THEATRICAL AS I WANT TO BE!'

JASMIN, AUSTRALIA

33

THE SECRET DOOR . . .

The Cairo Marriott's nightclub fell into darkness. Seated throughout its many lavish tiers were executives in designer suits, gold merchants and Arab sheikhs visiting from the Gulf. Originally a grand palace built for Napoleon Bonaparte, whose army exiled the dancing girls of Cairo, the site is now renowned for the best dancing in the Middle East.

A dimming of lights brought a lull in the laughter and chatter, and in the stillness of the summer night, the heady scent of jasmine wafted in from the palatial gardens. Even in the blackness, the women's gold jewellery glinted like faraway stars. A pendent silence teased the audience. Then a formal, resonating Egyptian voice announced, 'Raqs el sharqi . . . Neni!'—an introduction drawing hearty applause.

Silence again. A violin cried out in the darkness and a flute answered its call. Slowly, the lights shone across the orchestra, growing brighter, and what had appeared in the gloom to be only a few musicians now grew to 40. After several bars from the orchestra, rivulets of melodies gathering apace, a drum roll began . . . drrrrrr, dom tak-tak, dom tak-tak. On the crest of a malfuf rhythm, Neni glided onto the stage—her lilac costume shimmering with every agile movement of her body. Heavy black hair and diaphanous chiffon veils caressed the air as she twirled from one end of the floor to the other. Tak! The tabla stopped, its final sharp beat commanding stillness. For a moment, the audience drew back its breath in anticipation before this dancer who had so far eluded their gaze with her bold, swift entrance. And for an instant she was still; her swift, winged greeting subdued to a quiet pose. With delicacy, she looked into the eyes of her audience.

The qanoon began its tremolando quiver. Darkness enveloped Neni, all but for a soft light illuminating the trembling flesh of her ample belly and hips. The dance had begun. The door had opened.

My first memories of Cairo—the live music, the dancer's sensitivity, the intangible radiance that spread among us—carried me where no amount of study and practice could have. In this experience I rediscovered the value of the lived moment, of every dance's actuality in a particular time and place, the life it is drawn from and returns to the givers, its value for those who participate, whether as performers or as audience. There was magnificence in this dance.

As the reflection of the city's lights shimmered on the eternal Nile, I began to understand the essence of Eastern bellydance. The people themselves hold the secret to this ancient art, and they are its key. As they feel, understand and engage with the music and sentiments of the songs, they teach us that surrendering to the music is the secret. And, for you, it will reveal itself as the magic ingredient that breathes life into your own performance, as you practise the movements.

That's why these words are perhaps the best way to close. If this book has given you a glimpse of the world of Middle Eastern dance, if you are charmed and want to learn more, you will find the secret door . . . your own. But here we have analysed enough.

Now let us enjoy!

Glossary

Amazigh	A North African tribe, widely known as Berbers. 'Amazigh' is the name the tribe calls themselves in their native language
Andalusian	Spanish/Moorish inspired dance with sweeping movements, half moon poses and traditionally performed in a pale coloured dress with long sleeves and turban
arghul	Arabic twin reed pipe, played like a flute
Assyut	Egyptian town known for its famous silver-embossed fabric
assyuti	silver-embossed fabric from Assyut, Egypt
Aswan.	southern Egypt, also known as Upper Egypt or Upper Nile
ayoub	rhythm
balad	Arabic term meaning 'country' or 'homeland'
baladi	style of dance popular throughout Egypt. Baladi is more refined than folkloric dance, but is deep seated and earthier than classical dance. It is usually performed in a kaftan or dress with a hip scarf and/or headscarf. The assyuti dress is popular attire for baladi. Downward hip moves are a prominent feature
bambi	Arabic for the colour pink, also refers to a coquettish style of baladi dance
bazouki	Greek lute, similar to an Arabic oud but with a longer neck and smaller body
bint al balad	Arabic term meaning 'girl of the country'
bourka	full face veil worn in the Middle East, made from either netting or opaque fabric
call-and-response	a musical term for conversation between instruments
Catal Huyuk	ancient town in Turkey where Neolithic art showing dance images has been excavated
Cengi	Turkish term for 'gypsy'
chiftetelli	traditional Greek and Turkish style of bellydancing and music. Performed in a two-piece costume, chiftetelli is a cabaret style of bellydance with many undulations and upward pelvic tilts

dabke	strong group dance performed with men only, or a combination of men and women, linking arms with footwork in sync. Performed in Lebanon, Syria and Jordan
danse du ventre	the French term for bellydance
daraba	Arabic, meaning 'to strike'
darbuka	Turkish or Arabic drum made from clay or metal with a skin cover
darj	Iranian (Persian) dance rhythm in 6/8 timing
djinn	Arabic name for spirits
dof	Arabic skin-covered tambourine without cymbals
doholla	largest of the Egyptian tablas (drums)
dom	the name given to the bass sound produced when striking the tabla (drum)
Druze	branch of Islam whose followers, mainly from Lebanon, Israel and Jordan, believe God incarnated himself as Fatmid caliph al-Hakim
dumbek	Turkish metallic drum
El Saiid	province also known as Upper Egypt
Eskendereya	the Egyptian name for the city of Alexandria in northern Egypt. Also, an Alexandrian dance performed with a milaya (a heavy shawl that was a popular fashion accessory in the 1940s), a bourka (a netted face veil) and a frilly knee-length dress with shreb-shrebs (clogs)
Fayoum Oasis	fertile farming province in north-west Egypt
fellaha	Arabic term for 'farm girl'
fellahi	festive fast-paced celebration dance of Egyptian farmers, where dancers use pots or dofs (tambourines) and dance in colourful floral-print kaftans with head pieces lined with pom-poms
figure-eights	bellydance move that traces a shape of a number eight
folk dance	traditional cultural dance of the people
galebeya	Arabic cotton kaftan

Ghawazee	Gypsies of Egypt, literally meaning 'invaders of the heart'. Also, a vibrant gypsy dance with finger cymbals and fast hip moves. The typical costume is a kaftan or shirt that is tight fitting on top, with wide skirts and pantaloons
hafla	Arabic term for 'party' or 'celebration'
jairk	fast Nubian rhythm often used in today's pop songs
Karsilama	Turkish folkdance, usually danced in a group and performed to a complex 9/8 rhythm with syncopated steps
katem	Arabic term for 'background', also a type of large round-based drum played between the knees sometimes called the 'katem'
kavala	Turkish reed flute, originally a shepherd's pastoral calling instrument
kawala	Arabic reed flute
khaleegee	dance from the Arabian gulf of refined, rhythmic footwork, hand gestures and hair flicking moves. Traditionally performed in a long gold-embroidered kaftan, which is held in the hands while dancing
khawals	gypsy men who dress as and impersonate female dancers
lokoum	term for the gelatinous dessert Turkish delight, also a type of Turkish bellydance move
maktoum	Arabic drum (also see katem)
malemma	head village woman, usually an older woman
malfuf	fast Arabic rhythm for the dancer's entrance
maqsoum	sprightly Arabic drum rhythm
Marmaris	cosmopolitan coastal city in south-west Turkey
masmoudi	rhythm
mastika	literally 'drinking song', this is a rather parodied version of fast Turkish dance, with many upward pelvic tilts and hip lifts
maya	an outward figure of eight bellydance move that means 'water' in Arabic
mazhar	large tambourine with cymbals

mervlana	Turkish term for the whirling dervish
milaya il'laff	a type of large veil used for an Egyptian dance from Alexandria
mizmar	Arabic horn played at festivals
nawari	Lebanese folk rhythm used for line group dances
Netumun	tomb of Pharaonic king of Thebes, famous for the excavated scene 'the Banquet' dated at 1400 BC
nay	Arabic or Turkish reed flute
nubian	sprightly folk dance from Nubia with African overtones, usually performed in a white cotton kaftan with colourful embroidered vest and cap
oriental	term for the classical style of bellydance in the Middle East
oud	Arabic lute with a large pear-shaped body and short neck
Ouled Naïl	earthy yet poised dance of the Ouled Naïl tribeswomen on the Algerian fringe, who fascinated travellers in the 1900s. Performed in a highly decorated tribal costume with heavy skirts, layered with coins
qanoon	Arabic zither made of walnut with 48 strings
rababa	ancient Arabic string instrument made from a coconut shell, similar to a violin
rakkass	Turkish term for 'dance'
rakkassa	Turkish term for 'dancer'. Also, a flamboyant cabaret bellydance performed in a two-piece costume with an emphasis on hip lifts and shimmies
raqs sharqi	Arabic term literally meaning 'dance of the East'. Also used to describe classical refined bellydance, usually in two-piece costume, with an emphasis on arm work, ballet-inspired turns and refined hip work. Dramatic and sensual with many changing moods, and often danced to orchestral pieces
reque	small tambourine with skin and cymbals
sagat	Arabic term for finger cymbals
Saiidi men's dance	from El Saiid, Upper Egypt, where men in kaftans use heavy canes in sprightly martial arts-like movements

santoor	instrument similar to a zither, but played with wooden mallets
saz	Turkish lute with a small pear-shaped body and very long slender neck
sha'bia	modern style of Egyptian street dancing
shamadan	dance, usually with baladi movements, with brass candelabra worn on the head
sharqi	eastern
sheb-sheb	shoes
siz	Turkish horn
tabla	drum
tabul	large double-sided bass drum
tak	the name given to the treble sound produced when striking the tabla
takht	Arabic name for an ensemble of woodwind and string instruments
taktib	the name of the stick and the men's cane dance of Upper Egypt
taqsim	improvised dance to emotive melodies
toura	extra large finger cymbals played in the orchestra
tremolando	quivering note with a vibrating quality, especially heard with strings
Tuareg	tribe of Moroccan Berbers also known as the 'blue people' because the indigo in their face veils and turbans would stain their skin
wahda el'kebira	spacious rhythm literally meaning 'the large one'
wahda wa noss	Arabic 4/8 rhythm with two distinct parts meaning 'one and a half' used in Egyptian baladi dance
zaar	Egyptian trance dance and spiritual cleansing ritual that involves shaking the body and flicking the hair
zaffa	Arabic term for wedding. Also, a characteristic rhythm for a wedding procession, involving percussionists, mizmar players and folkloric dancers
zills	Turkish term for finger cymbals